St Josemaría Escrivá

LETTER 29

Dei amore, 9 January 1959

St Josemaría Escrivá

LETTER 29

Dei amore, 9 January 1959

ON THE WORK OF SAINT GABRIEL IN OPUS DEI

SCEPTER

London – New York

This edition of *St Josemaría Escrivá: Letter 29* is published:
in England by Scepter (U.K.) Ltd., 21 Hinton Avenue, Hounslow TW4 6AP; e-mail: scepter@pobox.com;
in the United States by Scepter Publishers Inc.,
info@scepterpublishers.org; www.scepterpublishers.org

Original title: *Josemaría Escrivá de Balaguer: Carta 29*

ISBN 978-1-910644-31-7 (paperback)

This edition is available for sale only in America.

Cover design and typeset by ISV Intermedia

Contents

INTRODUCTION

In 2020, the *Istituto Storico San Josemaría Escrivá*, began to publish the *Collection of Letters* that the founder of Opus Dei had written throughout his life, dealing with central aspects of the charism and history of this institution. To date, two volumes have been published, with a total of eight *Letters*. The present volume anticipates the publication of *Letter* 29 (dated 9 January 1959) in that collection.

Since this text is previously unpublished in English and largely unknown even to many members of Opus Dei, the aim has been to highlight the text itself, reducing the notes to the indispensable minimum so as not to distract the reader. The explanations that have been introduced serve to clarify aspects which, in the editor's opinion, may not be immediately comprehensible to everyone, or to contextualise statements which, when they were written sixty years ago or more, perhaps had a meaning different from today's, due to distance in time or semantic evolution. It is left to specialists who wish to gloss on, deepen in or carry out any theological-spiritual exegesis of these texts, to do so elsewhere, since – as we have said – that is not the object of this publication.

As with other writings of the founder addressed to members of Opus Dei, most of St Josemaría Escrivá's teachings have universal value, and will be of interest to a wide audience, especially with regard to the vocation of lay people to holiness.

In this English edition,* we have chosen to use both the original title and the corresponding Letter Number. Thus, for example, "*Dei amore,* 9 January 1959", [*Letter 9 January 1959*], or "Letter 29". Some readers will find it easier to associate the content of a particular *Letter* with its Latin name or date.

St Josemaría used Sacred Scripture in the Latin version of the Vulgate then in force. After quoting a text in Latin, he might translate it or paraphrase it. Where he does neither, we have usually chosen to include a translation in the main text. Where his paraphrase differs markedly, the English translation is shown as a footnote. All English translations are from the ESV-CE (English Standard Version – Catholic Edition).

5 August 2023

(65th anniversary of St Josemaría Escrivá's first Mass in the English-speaking world)

* To avoid awkwardness in translation, the masculine is often used, when in fact the original text addresses both men and women

Letter 29

Dei amore, 9 January 1959

1. Context and history

There is no information about the drafting process of this *Letter*, which came off the printing press run by women of Opus Dei in Villa Sacchetti (Rome) in January 1966, together with fourteen other similar ones, dealing with various topics, such as humility, the apostolic mission of the members of Opus Dei in the world, the sanctification of work, the juridical itinerary of the Work, apostolate in the field of education, priests in Opus Dei, the work of St Michael, etc.

The date of the *Letter*, 9 January 1959, is undoubtedly close to the time when it was written, but it is not possible to be more precise about exactly when St Josemaría wrote it. After it was printed, copies were sent to various countries on 21 January 1966.

St Josemaría had dealt in depth with this subject in 1950, when writing the *Instruction on the work of St Gabriel* – the fourth of his *Instructions* – which he had begun in 1935. In 1950, Opus Dei received the definitive approval of its Constitutions, in which the figure of supernumeraries was described in considerable detail, substantially as we know it today. Their vocation to holiness and apostolate in civil society, their means of personal and collective formation, the practice of the various virtues and the life of prayer, the call to illuminate all upright earthly realities with the light of Jesus Christ, are outlined in those Constitutions with features that are reflected today in the lives of thousands of women and men, married and single, who are supernumeraries of Opus Dei.

In fact, almost everything in the 1950 Constitutions concerning supernumeraries had been incorporated two years earlier, in an important revision of Opus Dei's statutes, which the founder presented on 2 February 1948 and which were approved by the Holy See on 18 March of that year. Up to that time, the statutory texts of Opus Dei (1941, 1943 and 1947) had dealt in a minimalist way with the figure of supernumeraries, for various reasons, but perhaps mainly because, as the founder himself acknowledged, it had not been possible to devote the necessary attention to this aspect of the Work. The development of Opus Dei, the possibility of having its own priests and members sufficiently trained and mature to take on this task, together with the approval of 1947, changed that perspective: St Josemaría now saw the long-awaited time had come to develop this type of member to its full extent.

The *Instruction* was very closely linked, therefore, to the statutory approval of the figure of supernumeraries, juridically united to Opus Dei with a true vocation, with "*a full dedication to the Lord*" in the Work, as St Josemaría said, even if they only carry out those apostolates that are compatible with their family and social circumstances. The *Instruction* dealt with all this in a simple, non-legal style, in a manner more in keeping with the formation of the future members. It reveals to them the spiritual and apostolic richness of the supernumerary vocation, and also the specific objective of the work of St Gabriel.

In 1962, after two failed attempts to change Opus Dei to a canonical framework different from secular institutes, which the founder considered inadequate in view of their evolution towards forms of consecrated life, St Josemaría set to work on his *Letters*. The first to be printed, and the shortest of them all, had precisely the purpose of communicating to his daughters and sons that Opus Dei could no longer be considered a secular institute.

This *Letter* was followed by a number of other short ones, which addressed the formative needs of the time, explaining aspects of the spirit and history of Opus Dei that the founder wished to emphasise, not only for those historical circumstances, but also with a view to leaving guiding and inspirational texts for future generations.

Little by little, these documents increased in number and length, until January 1966, when the present *Letter* was printed. Why did he feel the need to write again on the subject of the work of St Gabriel, to which he had devoted a lengthy document like the *Instruction* only a few years earlier? There are several hypotheses.

In the first place, there is a certain duplication between *Instructions* and *Letters* with regard to the three works into which Opus Dei is structured: the work of St Michael, the work of St Gabriel and the work of St

Raphael. Each has an *Instruction* and a *Letter* dedicated to it. For some reason, St. Josemaría felt it necessary to have two long texts on each of these subjects. His initial idea was that the *Instructions* would be a practical guide for developing each of these works, while the *Letters* would simply be devoted to the same themes, or to a specific one he wished to emphasise, without following a systematic order. This is what seems to be deduced from the following paragraph – and others like it – contained in one of the *Letters*:

> There are writings of mine, the *Instructions*, which, by their nature, I am not holding back: I give them to you at once, so that you may meditate on them and put them into practice. They highlight aspects of our doctrine, of what is proper to the spirit of the Work, and some other circumstantial elements which are not perennial. The *Letters*, on the other hand, can wait, and sometimes must wait: I do not know when the one I am writing now will reach you. You do not need these documents, at least not immediately, because all the positive things you are already experiencing, and experiencing them well. The rest – I repeat – belongs to our internal history, and this is not the time to do it.[1]

If one compares the content of the *Instruction on the work of St Gabriel* and the present *Letter*, one notices clear differences. The former was written when the activities with those not called to celibacy had just begun to take off, so to speak. In 1947-1948 the supernumerary vocation had been defined in detail, the first requests for admission had been received, and the first

[1] *Letter 29 December 1947–14 February 1966*, 13 [Letter 13, 13]

residential course had taken place. In 1950, therefore, although the number of members in this category had increased, it was practically just beginning and it was necessary to explain in detail the nature of this vocation; how the pastoral care of these people was to be organised; what virtues they were to practise; what their apostolates were; how their formative activities were to be carried out; what kind of evangelising activity they were called to in civil society, and how their Christian influence could be brought to bear, etc. At some points in the *Instruction*, the founder gets down to very practical and detailed advice.

The present *Letter* has a different perspective from that of the 1950 *Instruction*. Although we do not know when he began it, we do know that he finished it at the end of 1965, when the world had changed a great deal, and even more radical social transformations were on the horizon. These would have repercussions in many dimensions of human life, first of all religious, but also moral and family life. He urgently needed to underline an aspect of St Gabriel's work which he had already alluded to in the *Instruction* but which he pays much more attention to here, namely, its evangelising role: not only is it meant to be a channel for personal apostolate, but it should also have a Christian influence on a world which is dramatically turning away from God, at least in the West. In this sense, as can be seen from reading it or in the summary of its contents which follows, these themes are predominant.

The *Letter* also addresses an issue which in 1950

was only alluded to in passing, but which by 1965 had become very topical for the founder. By 1962 St Josemaría had become convinced that it was necessary for Opus Dei to abandon its juridical configuration as a secular institute as soon as possible, so as to guarantee the full secularity of the vocation to Opus Dei. If there is one thing that characterises the *Letters* of St Josemaría which came off the press in 1962, it is his reiterated insistence on the secularity of the members, on the difference between their vocation and that of the religious, on aspects such as their freedom, their full insertion into the world, etc. These were themes that he did not need to emphasise in 1950. In the *Letter* we are commenting on they come up frequently, and the intention is clear: to mark a before and an after, to establish for ever the genuine doctrine of Opus Dei about the lay nature of the vocation of supernumeraries.

One further reason the founder may have had for writing this *Letter*: when it came out, in the mid-1960s, the work of St Gabriel was undergoing a great expansion in various countries. To have a text like this at that time could have been very useful for the formation of the people who had to direct or give formation to supernumeraries and also to pass on to them the founder's teaching on the many aspects dealt with in this text. Public opinion on some of them, such as questions of matrimonial morality, had changed profoundly since 1950, and was highly topical in 1966, when the *Letter* appeared, as will be seen in the notes to those paragraphs.

2. Content

St. Josemaría begins his *Letter* by explaining that the salvation brought by Christ is destined for all men and women without exception. But, although His redemption is superabundant, it must be noted that many do not know Christ and that evil has prospered in the world: "In the field that God made for himself on earth, which is Christ's inheritance, there are weeds. And not merely weeds, but weeds in abundance!" (no. 3), he writes. Faced with this reality, these pages are a call not to remain indifferent but to take part in the redemption with Christ. It is necessary, he says, to act like the leaven in the dough, with a slow and constant action, so as to divinise people (nos. 1-9).

It is in this context of wide apostolic horizons – he continues in nos. 10-15 – that the work of St Gabriel is located, with which "we fill all the activities of the world with a supernatural content which, as it spreads, will contribute effectively to solving the great problems of mankind" (no. 10). This is a key point in the *Letter*: the impact of St Gabriel's work is not limited to improving the Christian life of those who participate in it, but leads, as a consequence of personal action, to animate and illuminate temporal realities and structures with the life and light of Christ. In this section he speaks of the vocation of supernumeraries, highlighting this evangelising and transforming projection: they are people of every type and social class who can have a Christian influence, both in the leading positions of society and at the most modest crossroads of life, with a diversified apostolate, which has all the specialisations that life itself offers. Hence the importance of the secular professional vocation, part of the supernumerary vocation, which, among other aspects, differentiates it from the apostolates carried out by other entities within the Church.

The central part (nos. 16-32) begins by dealing with the relationship between holiness and personal apostolate. It then goes on to develop further the main theme of this *Letter*, which was already very much present in the previous section. The professional and apostolic action is not only directed towards carrying out one's apostolate with individuals, but is fused together so that the member of Opus Dei aspires to build a more just and Christian society. To this end, the founder exhorts them to love the world and to be fearlessly present in all human activities and organisations. Without irresponsibly leaving the field open to the enemies of God and, at the same time, without acrimony: "Our attitude, my children, should be one of understanding, of love. Our action and approach is not directed against anyone, it can never have tones of sectarianism. We strive to drown evil in an abundance of good" (no. 25). Characteristic of Opus Dei's way of working is "a very great love for all people, a heart open to all their concerns and problems, and a broad understanding that leaves no room for discrimination or excluding others" (no. 26). But, St Josemaría insists, a Christian cannot rest on his laurels: while remaining active, serene, realistic, we must strive "to Christianise all the activities of the world, and place Christ at the summit of all human activities!" (no. 28). In this area he underlines the importance of teaching the Gospel message to all peoples.

A brief section (nos. 33-37) is devoted to a gloss on some characteristics of the formation of supernumeraries. He dwells especially on the freedom which must inform this formation. Freedom also to develop in the broad field of personal and professional action and of the options open to opinion: "Freedom, my children," he declares. "Don't ever expect the Work to tell you what to do in temporal affairs" (no. 36). He exhorts each one to seek the solutions which, in conscience, one considers most appropriate to solve temporal problems. He complains that in the Church there are those, driven by clericalism, who do not understand and respect this freedom.

There follows another short section (nos. 38-42) in which he sets out other characteristics of the apostolate of supernumeraries, men and women: it is not an ecclesiastical task; it must be imbued with humility; it is exercised in the sphere of civic duties and rights, because the vocation has a "fully secular character" (no. 41). He thus insists again on the need to be present, as Christian leaven, in human affairs and specifically, if the opportunity arises, in public life, bearing in mind the importance of civil legislation in shaping the lives of men and women in matters of moral relevance.

After a brief reference to cooperators (no. 43), he dwells on some specific apostolates, such as that of announcing the Gospel message to public opinion through the mass media (nos. 44-46); the apostolate of entertainment; involvement in finance and in the various fields of economics and politics (nos. 47-52)

A final section (nos. 53-58) is devoted to family life and marriage, providing criteria for the holy exercise of conjugal duties at a time when sexual permissiveness was making inroads, as was the contraceptive mentality and divorce. The *Letter* ends with some concluding words which exhort members to commit themselves to the vocation they have received, supported by the awareness of their divine filiation (nos. 59-60).

Letter 29

Rome, 9 January 1959

1. God in his love has chosen us, my beloved daughters and sons, to undertake this ever young and new path of the Work, this human and supernatural adventure, which is co-redemption with Christ, a close and intimate participation in Jesus' impatient longing to spread the fire that he came to cast on the earth.[1] God in his love has chosen us

With his cross and his triumph over death, he tore up the decree condemning men[2] and ransomed them all at the immense and infinite price of his own blood: *empti enim estis pretio magno,*[3] we have been bought at a great price. For all humanity without exception, he opened up the possibility of a new life, of being reborn in the Spirit, of beginning a life of victors who can exclaim: *If God is for us,* The price of our redemption

[1] Cf. Luke 12:49.

[2] Cf. Col 2:14.

[3] *Empti enim estis pretio magno. Glorificate et portate Deum in corpore vestro* (1 Cor 6:20): "For you were bought with a great price. So glorify and bear God in your body." Cf. 1 Pet 1:18-19.

who can be against us? He who did not spare his own Son but gave him up for us all, how will he not also with him graciously give us all things? ... For I am sure that neither death nor life, nor angels nor rulers, nor things present nor things to come, nor powers, nor height nor depth, nor anything else in all creation, will be able to separate us from the love of God in Christ Jesus our Lord.[4] What a splendid hymn of security, of plenitude, of godliness, one which our poor human clay could never have dreamt of intoning!

Not all accept salvation

2. But while he offers his salvation to all men and women without distinctions of nation, race, language or walk of life,[5] our Lord does not force anyone to accept it. He leaves men free. Sometimes men do not want that salvation, and they oblige Jesus to permit their low and selfish excuses, their rejections – *habe me excusatum*[6] – of his loving invitation to take part in the great banquet.

Few who hold the true doctrine of Christ

It is pitiful to see that, after twenty centuries, there are so few people in the world who call themselves Christians and that, among those who do call

---

[4] *Quid ergo dicemus ad haec? Si Deus pro nobis, quis contra nos? Qui etiam proprio Filio suo non pepercit, sed pro nobis omnibus tradidit illum: quo modo non etiam cum illo omnia nobis donavit?... Certus sum enim quia neque mors, neque vita, neque angeli, neque principatus, neque virtutes, neque instantia, neque futura, neque fortitudo, neque altitudo, neque profundum, neque creatura alia poterit nos separare a caritate Dei, quae est in Christo Iesu Domino nostro* (Rom 8:31-32 and 38-39).

[5] Cf. Gal 3:28; Col 3:11.

[6] Cf. Luke 14:15-24: "Please excuse me."

themselves Christians, there are so few who hold the true doctrine of Jesus Christ. I have told you sometimes about the man who was looking at a globe – he wasn't bad at heart but he had no faith – and he said to me, "Look, from north to south, from east to west, look." "What do you want me to look at?" I asked. And this was his reply, "The failure of Christ. So many centuries trying to put his doctrine into men's hearts, and look at the results: there are no Christians."

Christ has not failed

I was overcome, at first, with sadness; but, immediately afterwards, with love and gratitude, because God has willed to make us free cooperators in his redeeming work. Christ has not failed: his doctrine and his life are constantly enriching the world. His redemption is sufficient and super-abundant, but he treats us like intelligent, free beings. He has arranged things so that, in a mysterious way, we may fulfil in our flesh – in our life – what is lacking in his afflictions, *pro corpore eius, quod est Ecclesia*.[7]

Co-redeemers

The redemption is still being carried out: and you and I are co-redeemers. It is worth while risking our whole life, and being willing to suffer, for love's sake, in order to bring forward the things of God

---

[7] *Qui nunc gaudeo in passionibus pro vobis, et adimpleo ea, quae desunt passionum Christi, in carne mea pro corpore eius, quod est Ecclesia* (Col 1:24): "Now I rejoice in my sufferings for your sake, and in my flesh I am filling up what is lacking in Christ's afflictions for the sake of his body, that is, the church."

and help him redeem the world, in order to co-redeem. As we consider this, we see that the time has come for you and me to cry out in praise of God: *laudationem Domini loquetur os meum, et benedicat omnis caro nomini sancto eius.*[8] May our mouth speak forth the praises of the Lord, and all creatures bless his holy name.

The weeds and the good wheat

3. We cannot forget, my children, that our Lord has said that his kingdom is not of this world.[9] By permitting the misuse of human freedom, he tolerated the fact that, up to the time of the harvest, weeds can grow along with the good wheat.[10] And evil has prospered! From the very cradle of the Church, even while the Apostles were still alive, there arose heresies and schisms. And then persecutions by pagans in the early times of Christianity, Islam, Protestantism, and now Communism. In the field God made for himself on earth, which is Christ's inheritance, there are weeds. And not merely weeds, but weeds in abundance!

Until the holy city, the new Jerusalem, comes down from heaven – a new heaven and a new earth[11] – there will be no truce in the battle that is being fought. It is a battle fought, on the one hand,

---

[8] *Laudationem Domini loquetur os meum; et benedicat omnis caro nomini sancto eius in saeculum, et in saeculum saeculi* (Ps 145[144]:21).
[9] Cf. John 18:36.
[10] Cf. Matt 13:24-30.
[11] Cf. Rev 21:1-2.

by the *Lord of lords and King of kings, and those with him are called and chosen and faithful*[12] and on the other, by the servants of the beast, and of *the son of perdition, who opposes and exalts himself above all that is called God or is object of worship, so that he takes his seat in the temple of God, proclaiming himself to be God.*[13]

Optimism founded on Christ

4. Our optimism is not a foolish or presumptuous optimism: it is realism. Therefore we cannot ignore the presence of evil in the world, nor fail to feel the pressing responsibility of having been called up by Christ, to battle alongside him in his beautiful battle of love and peace.

Three expressions of the presence of evil in the world

Some years ago, in a spiritual retreat I gave your brothers, I had them take a look at the situation of the world, which has not changed very much since then. Speaking in a graphic way, I told them to contemplate the red stain that is spreading rapidly

---

12 *Hi cum Agno pugnabunt, et Agnus vincet illos: quoniam Dominus dominorum est, et Rex regum, et qui cum illo sunt, vocati, electi, et fideles* (Rev 17:14): "They will make war on the Lamb, and the Lamb will conquer them, for he is Lord of lords and King of kings, and those with him are called and chosen and faithful."

13 *Ne quis vos seducat ullo modo: quoniam nisi venerit discessio primum, et revelatus fuerit homo peccati, filius perditionis, qui adversatur, et extollitur supra omne, quod dicitur Deus, aut quod colitur, ita ut in templo Dei sedeat ostendens se tamquam sit Deus* (2 Thess 2:3-4): "Let no one deceive you in any way. For that day will not come, unless the rebellion comes first, and the man of lawlessness is revealed, the son of destruction, who opposes and exalts himself against every so-called god or object of worship, so that he takes his seat in the temple of God, proclaiming himself to be God." Cf. Rev 13:1-17.

over the earth, demolishing everything, trying to destroy even the slightest supernatural meaning. And the advance of another great wave of sensuality – forgive me for saying it – of imbecility, because men have a tendency to live like animals.

Then I pointed out for them yet another colour which is spreading and spreading, especially in Latin countries, and in a more hypocritical way in other nations. This is an anticlerical environment – the bad kind of anticlericalism – which seeks to relegate God and the Church to the sphere of conscience or, putting it in clearer terms, which wants to relegate God and the Church to the private sphere, so that the fact of having faith is not manifested in public life. I am not exaggerating. These three dangers are constant, evident and aggressive.

5. You cannot shut your eyes to this reality, since to do so would be an intolerable dereliction of duty. I say this, not for you to be filled with a passive, inert pessimism, but to be set on fire and filled with the holy impatience of Christ who, with rapid step, going ahead of his disciples – *praecedebat illos Iesus*[14] – made his last journey to Jerusalem,

---

[14] *Erant autem in via ascendentes Ierosolymam: et praecedebat illos Iesus, et stupebant: et sequentes timebant. Et assumens iterum duodecim, coepit illis dicere quae essent ei eventura* (Mark 10:32): "They were on the road, going up to Jerusalem, and Jesus was walking ahead of them. And they were amazed, and those who followed were afraid. And taking the twelve again, he began to tell them what was to happen to him."

to be baptised with a baptism that his spirit had been continually urging on him.[15]

Possumus!

When you hear our Lord's invitation, *Can you drink the chalice I am to drink, and be baptised with the baptism I am to receive?*[16] may this ringing, youthful and daring proclamation be always on your lips and in your souls: *possumus!*[17] – we can!

We cannot not remain indifferent in the presence of evil

Even though they are always serene with the serenity of their divine filiation, the children of God in his Work cannot remain indifferent at the sight of a world which is not Christian or even human. Many people have not yet attained the living conditions at the temporal level which would permit the development of the spirit. They are, as it were, insensitive to anything that is not carnal. The words of Scripture can be applied to them: they are *sensual men, devoid of the Spirit.*[18] What St Paul lamented is fulfilled in these poor souls: *animalis autem homo non percipit ea quae sunt Spiritus Dei,*[19] these poor creatures do not see the spiritual light, they do not discern the things which pertain to the spirit of God.

6. But turn your eyes to those nations which

---

[15] Cf. Luke 12:50.

[16] Mark 10:39.

[17] Mark 10:38.

[18] *Hi sunt qui segregant semetipsos, animales, Spiritum non habentes* (Jude 19): "It is these who cause divisions, worldly people, devoid of the Spirit."

[19] 1 Cor 2:14.

Human progress and spiritual growth

have attained an almost incredible growth in culture and progress, and which, in just a few years, have brought about a technical evolution which provides them a high level of material well-being. The findings of their research – and it is wonderful to see how God assists the human mind – should have led them closer to God because insofar as those things are true and good they proceed from God and lead to him.

Nevertheless, it isn't so: neither have they become more human, in spite of their progress. And they cannot be, for if the divine dimension is lacking, man's life, regardless of the material perfection it attains, is an animal life. Only when man opens himself to the religious dimension does he succeed in his striving to be distinguished from beasts. From a certain point of view, religion is the greatest rebellion of man, who does not want to be an animal.

Christ, Alpha and Omega, the beginning and the end

In the religious realm, my daughters and sons, there is no progress, there is no possibility of advancing further. The pinnacle of that development has been given to us already: it is Christ, Alpha and Omega, the beginning and the end.[20] Hence, in the spiritual life there is nothing left to

---

[20] *Et dixit mihi: factum est, ego sum alpha et omega: initium et finis. Ego sitienti dabo de fonte aquae vitae, gratis* (Rev 21:6): "And he said to me, It is done! I am the Alpha and the Omega, the beginning and the end. To the thirsty I will give from the spring of the water of life without payment."

be invented. The only thing open to us is to struggle to become identified with Christ, to be other Christs – *ipse Christus* – to fall in love with Christ and to draw our life from him who is the same yesterday as today and will be the same forever: *Iesus Christus heri et hodie, ipse et in saecula*.[21] Do you understand now why I repeat to you again and again that I have no other recipe to give you but this one: personal sanctity? There is no other way, my children, there is no other way.

7. There is need of yeast, a leaven that will divinise men and, in making them divine, will make them at the same time truly human. Even many of those who regard themselves as Jesus' disciples, even those who present themselves officially as devout, are in need of yeast. Leaven makes the dough tender, light and spongy, it transforms it, making it into nourishing food. Without yeast, the flour and water would produce nothing but a tough, indigestible, unwholesome lump.

Yeast to divinise mankind

God our Lord, in the midst of the great desertions, has always kept for himself a remnant of faithful people to act in the dough like leaven. *A remnant will return, the remnant of Jacob, to the mighty God. For though your people Israel be as the sand of the sea, only a remnant of them will return;*[22] the remaining fruit is left on the olive-tree when it is shaken, *when*

Those who act as leaven are always few

[21] Heb 13:8.

[22] Is 10:21-22.

the gleaning is over,[23] said the prophets. *So too at the present time,* wrote St Paul to the Romans, *there is a remnant, chosen by grace.*[24] Jesus used just a few people as leaven: that group of holy men and holy women, who cooperated with the first ones, in whose hearts he had carried out a marvellous sowing.

8. I used to point out to your first brothers that we were few in number. And with absolute conviction, I used to say to them, "All the better! Have we multitudes confronting us? But we are united by love. And they, although apparently united, are in fact disunited, because what brought them together was hatred: hatred which has always existed, the hatred which sprouts from a selfish life, from the eternal struggle of creatures rebelling against their Creator." And I used to add, "Do we want there to be more of us? Then let us be better!"

Yeast acts unhurriedly

My dear children, yeast does not produce its effect brusquely, or violently or partially, but slowly, unhurriedly, by an intrinsic power which acts on the whole dough. And you can see how this yeast has acted. Those few of the first hour, who had faith in God and in this poor sinner, have been an effective leaven, through the power of their supernatural life, their work and their joyous spirit of sacrifice. And by God's grace, we are now a

---

[23] *Quomodo si paucae olivae, quae remanserunt, excutiantur ex olea: et racemi, cum fuerit finita vindemia* (Is 24:13): "As when an olive tree is beaten, as at the gleaning when the grape harvest is done."
[24] Rom 11:5.

multitude, and you act in the same way, as a leaven, spread out almost worldwide.

9. For years, I was inflamed with love for God by the thought of Jesus' eagerness to set the world ablaze with his fire. I couldn't contain the irrepressible ardour that welled up within me, making me cry out with the same words the Master used: *Ignem veni mittere in terram, et quid volo nisi ut accendatur?... Ecce ego, quia vocasti me;*[25] I have come to set fire to the earth and what will I but that it be enkindled? ... Here I am, for you have called me.

Ignem veni mittere in terram

All my children are called to feel this magnanimous desire to put all their efforts, with whatever sacrifice is needed, into activating people's stifled and numbed energies in the service of God, and to make our Lord's cry their own: *misereor super turbam,*[26] with compassion for the multitude.

Magnanimous desire to serve all souls

No one in Opus Dei can rest content without feeling troubled by the depersonalised crowds: a drove, a flock, a herd, as I once called them. How many noble passions there are, under their apparent indifference, how many possibilities! We must serve everyone, laying our hands on each of them, as Jesus did – *singulis manus imponens*[27] – to bring them back to life, to heal them, to enlighten their

---

[25] Luke 12:49; 1 Sam 3:9. On several occasions St Josemaría alluded to this fact, which appears in his *Intimate Notes*, 1741 (16 July 1934).

[26] Mark 8:2: "I have compassion on the crowd."

[27] Luke 4:40: "he laid his hands on every one of them".

minds and strengthen their wills, so they can be useful! And then we will make of the flock, an army; of the drove, a band of followers; and bring out of the herd those who do not want to be unclean.

The Work already has the aroma of a ripe field

Today the Work has the aroma of a ripe field,[28] and, seeing the fruitfulness of the apostolate, we don't need faith to realise that God has blessed our work abundantly. Years ago, in my prayer, giving thanks to God, I serenaded the Work with a song from my homeland: *Capullico, capullico, / ya te estás volviendo rosa: / ya se está acercando el tiempo / de decirte alguna cosa* – "Little bud, little bud, / you are already becoming a rose. / Now the time is drawing near / to whisper something in your ear." My children, today you have in your hands some really beautiful, splendid roses, though they may have thorns. Now is the moment not to fall asleep, but to be vibrant, so as to gather up – and hand over to Jesus and to his Holy Church – the harvest that has been won with so much effort.

The Work of St Gabriel gives a Christian meaning to the whole of society

10. All our apostolic work aims directly to give a Christian meaning to society. But with the St Gabriel apostolate we fill all the activities of the world with a supernatural content which, as it spreads, will contribute effectively to solving the great problems of mankind.

Among the Supernumeraries there is the full range of social backgrounds, professions and jobs.

[28] Cf. Gen 27:27.

All kinds of circumstances and situations are sanctified by my children, men and women, who within their own state in life and situation in the world dedicate themselves to seeking Christian perfection with a *fullness of vocation*.

The fullness of the Supernumerary vocation

I say with "fullness of vocation" because, in the circumstances where God in his providence has placed them, they strive to respond with complete generosity to what the Lord asks of them in calling them to his Work: unconditional service, as responsible Catholic citizens, to the Holy Church, to the Roman Pontiff and to all souls.

Vocational meaning of marriage

Most of my Supernumerary daughters and sons live in the married state and for them conjugal love and duties are part of their divine vocation. Opus Dei has made marriage a divine path, a vocation. For more than thirty years I have been striving to make people aware of the vocational meaning of marriage. And, while teaching – this is not just something I say, it has been defined by the Church[29] – that virginity and also perfect chastity are superior to marriage, we have exalted marriage to the point of making it a vocation. How frequently I have seen a couple's eyes light up when, having thought that their noble and clean love was incompatible with dedication to God, they heard me say that "marriage is a divine path on earth!" I will come back to this point later on.

---

[29] *it has been defined by the Church*: Council of Trent, session 24, canon 10, 11 November 1563. See also note to §53.

Nicodemus and Joseph of Arimathea

11. Among Christ's disciples, the whole of the society of his times was represented: common folk and influential individuals alike. I have often drawn your attention to those two disciples: Nicodemus, a doctor of the law and a leading man, perhaps a member of the Sanhedrin; and Joseph of Arimathea, a rich man, belonging to the lay aristocracy of the supreme tribunal in Jerusalem. They acted discreetly and quietly. In public life they were true to the commands of their conscience.[30] And when the difficult hour came, they were brave and bold and did not hide.[31] I have always thought, and have told you, that if those two men were alive today they would understand the vocation of Supernumeraries in Opus Dei very well.

People from all walks of life

As with the first followers of Christ, so too among our Supernumeraries the whole of today's society is present, and it will always be so. There are intellectuals and businessmen; professional people and craftsmen; entrepreneurs and workers;

---

[30] *Et ecce vir nomine Ioseph, qui erat decurio, vir bonus et iustus, hic non consenserat consilio et actibus eorum* (Luke 23:50-51): "Now there was a man named Joseph, from the Jewish town of Arimathea. He was a member of the council, a good and righteous man, who had not consented to their decision and action."

[31] *Audacter introivit (Ioseph ab Arimathaea) ad Pilatum et petiit corpus Iesu* (Mark 15:43): "(Joseph of Arimathea) took courage and went to Pilate and asked for the body of Jesus." *Venit autem et Nicodemus, qui venerat ad Iesum nocte primum, ferens mixturam myrrhae et aloës, quasi libras centum* (John 19:39): "Nicodemus also, who earlier had come to Jesus, came bringing a mixture of myrrh and aloes, about seventy-five pounds' weight."

diplomats and people engaged in commerce, agriculture, finance and the arts; journalists, people in the theatre world, in films, the circus and sports; young and old, healthy and sick. It is an unorganised organisation, as wonderful as life itself. It is a true and authentic specialisation in the apostolate, because all honest and noble human vocations become apostolic and divine.

Unorganised organisation

We are interested in people from all professions and positions, from all social conditions, from the most diverse situations that exist or ever could exist, in this interweaving of mutual services that makes up society. This whole ensemble of living human interrelations needs to be permeated by the leaven of Christ.

All activities contribute to the work of redemption

12. Notice, my children, that we don't single out some professions or social conditions above the rest.[32] The value we seek in all of them, without

[32] *we don't single out some professions or social conditions above the rest*: One of the specific aims of Opus Dei, St Josemaría pointed out, is the Christian influence among intellectuals, because of its repercussion on the rest of society. But from the first years of its foundational activity "we are for the crowds: we can't ever turn our back on the masses" (Letter from Josemaría Escrivá to Mgr Francisco Morán, Vicar General of Madrid, Burgos, 4 April 1938) is a statement which resounds. In the earliest documentation we have, we can perceive his desire to reach workers, shop assistants, artists, nurses, etc., people of all professions and social conditions, among whom he would find people willing to join Opus Dei. For example, in *Intimate Notes*, 373 (November 1931), we read: "With God's help and the approval of Father Confessor, I will soon try to gather together a small group of select workers".

discrimination or class mentality, is what they can do for the service of the community, so that we raise up and give importance even to jobs which are looked down upon by some in society. All of these jobs work together for the temporal good of the whole of humanity. If they are done with perfection and for a supernatural motive – if they are spiritualised – they also cooperate in the divine work of Redemption and foster fraternity among all people, making them feel that they are members of the great family of God's children.

In one's own surroundings

We don't take anyone out of their place. Right there in the circumstances in which the Lord has called them, each and everyone has to sanctify themselves and to sanctify their surroundings, that human sphere to which they are linked, through which their existence in the world is justified. In this too we have the same outlook as the first Christians.

Remember what St Paul wrote to the faithful in Corinth: *Each one should remain in the condition in which he was called. Were you a slave when called? Do not be concerned about it. (But if you can gain your freedom, avail yourself of the opportunity.) For he who was called in the Lord as a slave is a freedman of the Lord. Likewise he who was free when called is a slave of Christ. You were bought with a price; do not become slaves of men. So, brothers, in whatever condition each was called, there let him remain with God.*[33]

---

[33] *Unusquisque in qua vocatione vocatus est, in ea permaneat. Servus vocatus es? non sit tibi curae: sed et si potes fieri liber, magis utere. Qui*

At all levels of society

13. At all levels of society, with God's grace, seek especially vocations to his Work among those people whose work places them in vital centres of human affairs, in those situations which are, so to speak, meeting points and crossroads where many people interact closely.

I am not talking only about the leading posts in a national or supranational community, from which, with a spirit of service, so much good can be done toward structuring society in accordance with Christ's demands, which guarantee true peace and authentic social progress.

Awakening people's consciences

I am also referring to other positions because they are just as important or even more so. These are professions or jobs in the sphere of smaller societies that, by their nature, are means of coming into contact with large numbers of people. From them, it is possible to form people's opinions in a Christian way, have an influence on their mentality and awaken their consciences, thanks to the constant desire to give doctrine which should characterise all God's children in his Work.

Accordingly, I have often told you that it is important – it is important to God our Lord – that there be vocations among people who hold key community posts: employees in borough councils

---

enim in Domino vocatus est servus, libertus est Domini: similiter qui liber vocatus est, servus est Christi. Pretio empti estis, nolite fieri servi hominum. Unusquisque in quo vocatus est, fratres, in hoc permaneat apud Deum (1 Cor 7:20-24).

(town hall personnel, city councillors, etc.), teachers, barbers and hairdressers, travelling salesmen, pharmacists, midwives, postal workers, waiters and waitresses, home helps, newspaper vendors, shop assistants, and so on.

Filling all the world's activities with a Christian spirit

Our work has to reach the most remote villages, because the desire for love and peace which moves us will fill all the activities in the world with a Christian spirit, by means of a capillary action which aims to give a Christian form to the living cells which together make up the larger communities. There should not be a single village without some Supernumerary there radiating *our spirit.* And, in keeping with our traditional way of acting, that son or daughter of mine will immediately try to pass on their holy concern to other people, and there will soon be a group of children of God in his Work there. And they will be properly looked after by means of whatever journeys and visits are necessary, so that the group doesn't shrivel up but continues vibrant and active.

A common denominator and a completely free numerator

Once the full extent of the diversity among the members of the Work is pointed out, our plurality can be understood perfectly. In matters of faith or in things having to do with the spirit of the Work, which are the lowest common denominator, we can say *we*. In everything else, everything temporal and everything which is left open to free opinion in theology – an immense, completely free numerator – none of my children can say *we*; you have to say *I, you, he*.

Breadth of the apostolic work

14. You know very well, my children, that our apostolic work does not have a specialised goal.[34] It contains every kind of specialisation, because it is rooted in the diversity of specialisations of life itself. It exalts and raises to the supernatural order all the many services which human beings render one another in the intertwined reality of human society and turns them into authentic work for souls.

The work of the religious

In recent centuries, religious of the active life, seeking to come closer to the world (although always from the outside), have tried to make their apostolates more specialised so as to infuse a Christian spirit into certain human undertakings: education, welfare work, and so on. This is praiseworthy work, but often it aimed not so much to shape or express the vocation proper to the

[34] *a specialised goal*: in the field of the lay apostolate, there was discussion for years as to whether it was better to follow the centralised and traditional model of Catholic Action, which was oriented towards the collaboration of the laity in parish activities, or the "specialised" model, which aimed at the insertion of the Catholic militant in the social problems of the environment. The latter gave rise to the so-called "specialised movements" (youth, workers, peasants, etc.), as in the Italian Catholic Action. When this *Letter* was written, this debate was still alive in Spain. For Opus Dei, according to its founder, any honest work or activity is an instrument of apostolate, which is why Opus Dei *contains every kind of specialisation* proper to life itself.

religious, as to make up for a lack of initiative on the part of Catholic citizens. Perhaps because their own Christian formation had been neglected, these Catholics did not feel they had a responsibility to Christianise temporal institutions.

The witness of consecrated life

The religious, however, did this task, which was not specific to their vocation, only in order to fill a gap. And in seeking to specialise, they found themselves limited, because there are many fields of human work which are perfectly honest and upright in themselves, but are utterly incompatible with the religious state. The principal common mission of the religious is to offer to the world, from which they have withdrawn with a holy intention, the witness of their consecrated life. Moreover, in many countries, including Catholic ones, the secularism of recent times, has been throwing the religious out of schools and charitable institutions, or at least has curtailed their activities that were not strictly religious.

In the apostolate of the Work, the laity, without being substitutes of any kind,[35] take full

---

[35] *without being substitutes of any kind*: St Josemaría wishes to point out that the apostolate of the laity of Opus Dei in the world is its *mission in the Church* and that it is articulated through the *secular professional vocation,* as he will say in the following paragraph. That is to say, it does not encroach on, nor is it considered better or superior to, the apostolate carried out self-sacrificingly by religious in the world: it is simply different, because it does not come from a vocation to the consecrated life but from Baptism, by which God calls all to be missionary disciples of Christ.

The apostolate of the Work is open to all areas of society

and responsible possession of the specific field God has indicated to them as the place for their mission in the Church. They carry out an apostolate whose possibilities of specialisation are unforeseeable because they are as many as the possibilities of human work and their roles in society. Without getting stuck in a rut, this apostolate is open to all the changes in structures that may take place over time in the way society is shaped.

At this point, I cannot avoid making the consideration that it is very difficult for the religious to feel they have an *ordinary secular professional vocation* – if they had had it, they wouldn't be religious – and that to train them to do professional jobs is difficult, expensive, *superimposed* and artificial. Under those conditions, I think only a very small number of people could reach the average professional standard attained by ordinary men and women.

Concern and responsibility for the entire Holy Church

15. For this reason we can say, my children, that there weighs upon us the concern and the responsibility for the entire Holy Church – *sollicitudo totius Sanctae Ecclesiae Dei* – and not just for this or that particular portion of it. Backing up the official responsibility of the Roman Pontiff and of the Right Reverend Ordinaries (a juridical responsibility, and theirs *de iure divino**), we serve the whole Church, with a responsibility which is not juridical,

* "by divine law" – *Trans.*

but rather spiritual, ascetical, born of love. We offer a service of a professional nature, as citizens who bring a Christian witness of example and doctrine to the furthermost reaches of civil society.

An Association which is universal in character

History shows the decisive role which universal organisations like the religious Orders and Congregations played in times that were difficult for the unity of the Church. With a vocation which is unrelated to that of the religious, we constitute an Association which is universal in character, with an internal hierarchy that is also universal. This internal hierarchy distinguishes us clearly[36] from what are called *apostolic movements* and makes us a cohesive and effective instrument for the service of the Church and the Roman Pontiff.

Effectiveness comes from personal holiness

16. Your effectiveness, my children, will be the result of your personal holiness, which will take shape in responsible deeds, that are not hidden in anonymity. Christ Jesus, the Good Sower, squeezes us like wheat in his wounded hand, soaks us in his blood, purifies us, cleanses us, makes us

---

[36] *distinguishes us clearly*: in reality, from the sociological and apostolic point of view, the differences with the movements are small; for St Josemaría, the diversity lies here in the universality of the pastoral phenomenon and of communion that Opus Dei represents, and also in the universality of its internal hierarchy. But this distinction does not mean a distance from the models of ecclesial renewal that many of the current movements have brought with them, with which Opus Dei shares the same yearning for holiness, evangelisation and service to the Church, and with which it maintains bonds of communion and fraternity.

drunk! And then, generously, he scatters us around the world, one by one, as is proper for his children in Opus Dei, for wheat is not sown by the sackful, but grain by grain.

Bearing abundant apostolic fruit

You are light in the Lord. Walk as children of light (for the fruit of light is found in all that is good and right and true).[37] It would be inconceivable, a falsehood, a double life, play-acting, if the life of a child of mine did not bear abundant apostolic fruit. I will tell you once more that such a child of mine would be dead, rotten!: *iam foetet.*[38] And, as you well know, what I do with corpses is bury them piously.

By engaging individually with your work colleagues, relatives, friends and neighbours, doing what I have often called the apostolate of friendship and trust, you will shake them out of their sleepiness and open up wide horizons to their selfish and bourgeois existence. You will complicate their lives, bringing them to forget about themselves and understand the problems of those around them. And, as you know from experience, you can be sure that by complicating their lives you are bringing them to *gaudium cum pace*, to joy and peace.

Image of the first Christians

This personal apostolate is not anarchical, because in doing it you are following the doctrinal or practical guidance of your Directors. As a result

---

[37] *Nolite ergo effici participes eorum. Eratis enim aliquando tenebrae: nunc autem lux in Domino. Ut filii lucis ambulate: fructus enim lucis est in omni bonitate, et iustitia, et veritate* (Eph 5:8-9).

[38] John 11:39: "by this time there will be an odour".

of it, if you carry it out constantly, you will create around you an atmosphere of serenity and will reproduce in your homes the image of the homes of the first Christian faithful.

Everything is a means for apostolate

As you practise that individual apostolate of yours, you try to draw the people you are in contact with to the collective means of spiritual and doctrinal formation organised by the Work: spiritual retreats, conferences, circles, and so on. You also draw them to spiritual direction with our priests. These means are most effective, indeed they are necessary, to complete the care of those souls you are looking after, making use of your professional life, of the place you occupy in the world, and your family circumstances. You make use of everything, because everything is a means for apostolate.

Giving a Christian focus to society

17. But you can't leave it at that. You can't be satisfied with bringing some of your relatives or friends to a recollection or putting them in contact with a priest of the Work. Your apostolic work doesn't end there. You must also realise fully that you are doing a most fruitful apostolate when you strive to orient in a Christian way the professions, institutions and human structures in which you move and work.

Trying to make those institutions and structures conform to the principles that govern a Christian conception of life means carrying out a very broad-based apostolate. By incarnating in that way the spirit of justice, you are ensuring that people can have the means to live in accord with their dignity, and you are helping many souls to respond personally, with the help of God's grace, to the Christian vocation.

When you hear me talking about justice, don't understand that word in a narrow sense. If people are to be happy, it is not enough to base their relationships on justice, which gives each their due in a cold manner. I am talking to you about charity, which presupposes and goes beyond justice, and about Christ's charity, which is not an official charity, but affection. Justice and charity

18. Therefore, in your action in society always avoid setting people against each other, because a Christian cannot have a class or caste mentality. Don't pull down some people in order to raise up others, for in that attitude there always lurks a materialistic outlook. Give everyone the opportunity to develop their personality and raise up their life through their work. Don't be satisfied with just avoiding hatred, because our common denominator must be to carry out a sowing of peace and love. Sowing peace and love

As you tackle your work, whatever it may be, examine yourselves, in God's presence, my children, to see if the spirit inspiring that work is truly a Christian spirit. And bear in mind that changes in historical circumstances – with the modifications that they introduce in the way society is shaped – can make something that was just and good at a given moment, cease to be so. Therefore, you must unceasingly exercise a constructive critical attitude, which will make it impossible for the paralysing and disastrous action of inertia to take effect.

Discovering the divine meaning of reality

19. We must win over for Christ every noble human value: *Whatever is true, whatever is honourable, whatever is just, whatever is pure, whatever is lovely, whatever is commendable, if there is any excellence, if there is anything worthy of praise, think about these things.*[39] Whatever reality appears in people's lives, we must bring it to God straight away and bring to light its divine meaning. That is why, as I've told you so many times, you must never lose the supernatural point of view. *Whatever you do, in word or deed, do everything in the name of the Lord Jesus, giving thanks to God the Father through him.*[40]

Ever in close contact with temporal structures, ever up to date, you will never need the *aggiornamento** people talk of today, because you will constantly have an understanding and responsible hope regarding the world in each epoch of its existence. You will demand that the values of freedom and the dignity of the human person be upheld, and will always be guided by a desire for unity and love in this service you give.

---

[39] *Quaecumque sunt vera, quaecumque pudica, quaecumque iusta, quaecumque sancta, quaecumque amabilia, quaecumque bonae famae, si qua virtus, si qua laus disciplinae, haec cogitate* (Phil 4:8).

[40] *Omne, quodcumque facitis in verbo aut in opere, omnia in nomine Domini Iesu Christi, gratias agentes Deo et Patri per ipsum* (Col 3:17).

* "bringing up to date" – *Trans.*

Love for the world dwells at the heart of Christianity

It has been God's will that by our vocation we should portray that optimistic view of creation, that *love for the world*, which dwells at the heart of Christianity. You should never lose your idealism, either in your work or in your commitment to build the temporal city. Yet at the same time, as Christ's disciples who *have crucified the flesh with its passions and desires,*[41] you strive to keep alive the sense of sin and generous reparation, in the face of the false optimisms of those *enemies of the cross of Christ,*[42] who measure everything in terms of human progress and activity.

Not forgetting sin

Such people commit the great sin of forgetting sin, which some even think they have removed altogether. They do not take into account that it forms part of the economy of redemption that the grain of wheat, in order to bear fruit, needs to be buried in the ground and die.[43] *Their end is destruction, their god is their belly, and they glory in their shame, with minds set on earthly things. But our citizenship is in heaven, and from it we await a Saviour, the Lord Jesus Christ, who will transform our lowly body to be like his glorious body, by the power that enables him even to subject all things to himself.*[44]

---

[41] *Qui autem sunt Christi, carnem suam crucifixerunt cum vitiis, et concupiscentiis* (Gal 5:24).

[42] *Multi enim ambulant, quos saepe dicebam vobis (nunc autem et flens dico) inimicos crucis Christi* (Phil 3:18).

[43] Cf. John 12:24.

[44] *Quorum finis interitus: quorum Deus venter est: et gloria in confusione ipsorum, qui terrena sapiunt. Nostra autem conversatio in*

Present in all human activities

20. With this sense of deep humility and relying for strength on the name of our God and not on the resources coming from our war chariots and horses,[45] be present *fearlessly* in all human activities and organisations, so that Christ may be present in them. As regards our way of working, I have applied to it those words of Scripture: *ubicumque fuerit corpus, illic congregabuntur et aquilae*,[46] because God our Lord will call us to strict account if, out of apathy or a desire to be comfortable, any of you freely choose not to intervene in the human projects and decisions on which the present and future of society depend.

Prudent not timid activity

It is very much part of your vocation to intervene prudently (and when I say prudently, I don't mean timidly), actively and discreetly, in the same way as the angels do, whose action is invisible but most effective, in the various local, national and international associations and corporations, whether they be public or not.

Promotion of all kinds of organisations

It would be a criminal omission if you were absent from assemblies, congresses, exhibitions, gatherings of scientists or workers, study courses, or, to put it simply, from any kind of initiative be it scientific, cultural, artistic, social, financial or

---

caelis est: unde etiam Salvatorem expectamus Dominum nostrum Iesum Christum, qui reformabit corpus humilitatis nostrae, configuratum corpori claritatis suae, secundum operationem qua etiam possit subiicere sibi omnia (Phil 3:19-21).

[45] Cf. Ps 20[19]:7.

[46] Matt 24:28: "Wherever the corpse is, there the vultures will gather".

sporting, etc. Sometimes it will be you yourselves who set them up; most of the time other people will have organised them and you will take part. But in any case you will try to ensure that you are not just present passively. You will feel the weight, the pleasant weight, of your responsibility, and you will try to make yourselves necessary, because of your high standing, your initiative and your drive, so that you set the right tone and infuse a Christian spirit into all those organisations.

and participating personally in official or private associations

21. Individually, without forming a group (which you cannot do anyway because every one of you has unlimited freedom in all temporal affairs), play an active and effective role in official or private associations, because they are never something indifferent as regards man's temporal and eternal well-being. Even a sports club or a collectors' club, just to give an example, may be used to do a lot of good or a lot of harm. It all depends on the people who run them or inspire them.

As I have told you, you work individually in those fields with personal freedom and responsibility. Nevertheless, realise that you are performing a service to God our Lord when you form around you other brothers or sisters, orienting them but obviously without trying to press them to change their personal inclinations, so that they can replace you or succeed you, and no part of the terrain is left unattended when you are no longer there.

Like the first Christians

22. That is how the first Christians acted. They did not have specific social or human programmes to carry out by virtue of their supernatural vocation. But they were permeated with a spirit, a way of looking at life and the world, that could not fail to have consequences in the society in which they lived.

Personal apostolate

With a personal apostolate similar to ours, they went about making converts and, during his captivity, Paul was already sending greetings to the churches from the Christians who lived in *Caesar's household*.[47] Are you not moved by that wonderful letter which the Apostle addresses to Philemon, a letter which is a living testimony of how the leaven of Christ – without directly intending it – had given a new meaning, through the influence of charity, to the structures of that society?[48]

We are a people of yesterday and yet we have filled every place belonging to you, cities, islands, castles, towns, assemblies, your very camps, your tribes, companies, palaces, senate, forum. We leave you your temples only.[49] Thus wrote Tertullian, little more than a century later.

---

[47] *Salutant vos omnes sancti, maxime autem qui de Caesaris domo sunt* (Phil 4:22): "All the saints greet you, especially those of Caesar's household."

[48] Cf. Philem 8-12; Eph 6:5 ff.; Col 3:22-25; 1 Tim 6:1-2; 1 Pet 2:18 ff.

[49] *Hesterni sumus et vestra omnia implevimus, urbes, insulas, castella, municipia, conciliabula, castra ipsa, tribus, decurias, palatium, senatum, forum: sola vobis reliquimus templa* (Tertullian, *Apologeticum*, 37).

Be filled with hope and encouragement

23. My children, be filled with hope and encouragement. Let us pursue unceasingly *what makes for peace and for mutual upbuilding.*[50] *Repay no one evil for evil, but give thought to do what is honourable in the sight of all. If possible, so far as it depends on you, live peaceably with all.* [51]

The children of darkness and the children of light

Recall often, as a spur to your conscience, our Lord's lament: *Filii huius saeculi prudentiores filiis lucis in generatione sua sunt;*[52] the children of darkness are more prudent than the children of light. These are hard words but true, since unfortunately they are borne out every day.

Meanwhile, the enemies of God and his Church move and get organised. With *exemplary* constancy, they prepare their cadres, they run schools where they form leaders and agitators and, with covert but effective action, they spread their ideas and bring to homes and to workplaces their seed that is destructive of all religious belief.

Marxism

My children, Marxism, in its various forms, is very active today, and in systematic fashion it aims to provide a scientific foundation for atheism. With incessant propaganda, not so much noisily as individually, it criticises every appearance or trace of religion and, setting itself up as a faith and

---

[50] *Itaque quae pacis sunt, sectemur, et quae aedificationis sunt, in invicem custodiamus* (Rom 14:19).

[51] *Nulli malum pro malo reddentes: providentes bona non tantum coram Deo, sed etiam coram omnibus hominibus. Si fieri potest, quod ex vobis est, cum omnibus hominibus pacem habentes* (Rom 12:17-18).

[52] Luke 16:8.

hope in earthly things, it seeks to replace true Faith and true Hope.

Those who lend a hand to God's enemies

I do not understand those people who call themselves Catholics and open their arms to Marxism, which the Church has so often condemned as being incompatible with her doctrine. They lend a hand to God's enemies, and treat Catholics who don't think as they do as enemies. A Catholic who ill-treats other Catholics and treats those who are not Catholic with apparent charity errs grievously, errs against justice. He is covering up his fault with false charity, because if charity is not properly ordered it ceases to be charity.

24. My children, advice from the enemy.[53] Be watchful and prudent, and do not fall asleep: *hora est iam nos de somno surgere,*[54] it is time to shake off laziness and sleepiness. Don't forget that there are

---

[53] *advice from the enemy*: a popular proverb that invites us not to follow the recommendation of those who seek our harm, however reasonable and opportune it may seem. The theme appears in the fable of the lion and the goat, attributed to Aesop, later taken up by other authors, such as Félix María Samaniego (1745-1801), where the phrase used by St Josemaría is quoted verbatim. In this fable (Book V, XXIII), the prudence of a dog is praised, which avoided being devoured, on discovering the insidiousness hidden in the suggestion of a crafty crocodile: "O what a learned old dog! / I venerate his feeling / In this of not following / advice from the enemy. Curiously, in §35 of this same *Letter*, St Josemaría uses it again, but in the opposite sense, as if to imply that those who do not think as we do can also express a helpful truth.

[54] Rom 13:11: "the hour has come for you to wake from sleep".

places on earth which once witnessed flourishing churches but are now a wasteland where Christ's name is never uttered. It would be too comfortable to try to justify that failure on the grounds that it falls within God's plans to write straight with crooked lines and that, in the end, God's cause always triumphs. It is true that Christ always triumphs, but, often, he does so in spite of us.

Complicating our lives

We should avoid a bellicose or aggressive spirit, *in hoc pulcherrimo caritatis bello,* in this beautiful war of charity, and in a spirit of understanding welcome everyone and work together with all men of good will, even with those who do not know or do not love Christ (without giving in to the errors they profess). However, do not forget that our Lord said, *Do not think that I have come to bring peace to the earth. I have not come to bring peace, but a sword.*[55] It is very easy to concentrate only on Jesus' meekness, and, because they disturb people's comfort-seeking and conformity, leave aside these words, which are equally divine, and with which he spurs us on to "complicate" our lives.

Defending the truth, drowning evil in an abundance of good

25. We human beings do not usually like telling and upholding the truth, because it is more comfortable to try to be accepted by all than to run the risk of falling out with somebody. Our attitude, my children, should be one of understanding, of

---

[55] *Nolite arbitrari quia pacem venerim mittere in terram: non veni pacem mittere, sed gladium* (Matt 10:34).

love. Our approach and action is not directed against anyone; it can never have tones of sectarianism. We strive to drown evil in an abundance of good. Our work is not negative, it is not *anti-anything*. It is affirmation, youthfulness, joy, and peace. But not at the cost of truth.

Thinking for oneself

Because we cultivate everyone's freedom of personality, we children of God in the Work are people who can think for ourselves. We don't take on board unquestioningly the clichés and catch-phrases which are all the rage – in fashion – at a given moment. Our formation teaches us to carry out a work of sifting, which retains what is valuable and leaves the rest behind. We will often have to swim against the current, as we have almost always done, opening up new channels and new paths. And we do so, not out of a desire to be original, but out of loyalty to Jesus Christ and his doctrine. The easy thing is to let oneself be carried along, but adopting easy positions often demonstrates also a lack of responsibility.

It is true that you must live at every moment among the people of your time, in tune with their mentality and customs. But at the same time *always be prepared to make a defence for the hope that is in you*[56] in Christ Jesus, so that not having to

---

[56] *Dominum autem Christum sanctificate in cordibus vestris, parati semper ad satisfactionem omni poscenti vos rationem de ea, quae in vobis est, spe* (1 Pet 3:15): "but in your hearts honour Christ the Lord as holy, always being prepared to make a defence to

adapt to your surroundings – since you are among your equals, your fellow men – does not mean that others cannot recognise you as disciples of Christ. What a great deal of sentimentalism, fear and cowardice there is in certain desires for adaptation!

Understanding without discriminating against or excluding others

26. My dear children, don't see anything behind my words except a very great love for all people, a heart open to all their concerns and problems, and a broad understanding that leaves no room for discrimination or excluding others. And understand that it is not fear which drives us, since we are not afraid of anything or anyone, not even of God, who is our Father. Rather it is a sense of responsibility that one day we shall have to render an account to our Lord of our co-redemptive mission, which urges us not to slacken – *caritas enim Christi urget nos*[57] – to be forever dissatisfied with what we have already achieved, and not to rest on our laurels!

Filling the world with love

Do not be slothful in zeal, be fervent in spirit,[58] make the most of your time,[59] because life is short: *As we have opportunity, let us do good to everyone, and especially to those who are of the household of faith.*[60]

---

anyone who asks you for a reason for the hope that is in you; yet do it with gentleness and respect."

57 2 Cor 5:14: "the love of Christ controls us".

58 *Sollicitudine non pigri, spiritu ferventes* (Rom 12:11).

59 Cf. Eph 5:16.

60 *Ergo dum tempus habemus, operemur bonum ad omnes, maxime autem ad domesticos fidei* (Gal 6:10).

Let us fill with love this poor world of ours, since it is ours; it is God's handiwork and he has given it to us as an inheritance: *dabo tibi gentes hereditatem tuam et possessionem tuam terminos terrae.*[61] Bear in mind that what is possible can be done by anyone, but God our Lord is asking us, and is giving us his grace as well, to do things that to you will seem impossible.

27. Don't remain in the realm of idealistic dreams. Be realistic. You see such immense things, so much scope for action, so much to be done and so many possibilities, that after gazing upon them, it could happen that you rest satisfied and forget the practical actions – *hodie, nunc* – which will make it possible for all those things someday to become a reality.

Keeping calm

In the middle of this marvellous combat, stay calm. To be entangled in worries is harmful. *Corripite inquietos,*[62] St Paul tells the Christian community of Thessalonica. *For we hear,* he said to them, *that some among you walk in idleness, not busy at work, but busybodies.*[63] And he gave them the only remedy, which is to fulfil our duty. When we do what we ought and put our hearts into what we are doing, we bring to reality God's great plans.

---

[61] Ps 2:8: *I will make the nations your heritage, and the ends of the earth your possession.*

[62] 1 Thess 5:14: "admonish the idlers".

[63] *Audivimus enim inter vos quosdam ambulare inquiete, nihil operantes, sed curiose agentes* (2 Thess 3:11).

Now such persons, the Apostle continued, *we command and encourage in the Lord Jesus Christ to do their work quietly and to earn their own living.*[64]

Christ at the summit of all human activities

28. How much our Lord expects from your constant, eager and enthusiastic work, even though frequently you will not "feel" eager or enthusiastic. Through this work you strive to Christianise all the activities of the world, and place Christ at the summit of all human activities!

The work of women Super-numeraries

This apostolate belongs especially to my Supernumerary sons and to my Supernumerary daughters too, who are so tenacious (sometimes more so than men) in bringing the salt and light of Christ to the milieu in which they move: their homes, their social life, and all their various professional jobs.

Judith

Re-read that Old Testament passage where Judith changed the minds of the people and their leaders when they were ready to surrender the city to enemy armies. The sacred text says: *When Judith heard the wicked words spoken by the people against the ruler… she summoned Uzziah and Chabris and Charmis, the elders of her city. They came to her, and she said to them, "Listen to me, rulers of the people of Bethulia! What you have said to the people today is not right... Who are you, who have put God to the test*

---

[64] *Iis autem, qui eiusmodi sunt, denunciamus, et obsecramus in Domino Iesu Christo, ut cum silentio operantes, suum panem manducent* (2 Thess 3:12).

this day, and are setting yourselves up in the place of God among the sons of men? You are questioning the Lord Almighty! But you will never know anything!"[65] This was a vigorous, bold rebuke, a model of how a supernatural, brave woman who is faithful to her conscience can influence the course of public life – normally quietly, discreetly yet most effectively – when Christ's interests need to be defended. Meditate also on the fortitude of the Blessed Virgin and those holy women, who stood firm at the foot of the Cross, when the men, in the hour of generalised cowardice, deserted.

Mary's fortitude

My daughters and sons, if you maintain this good spirit, what the Acts say about Jesus' Apostles will be applicable to yourselves today: *Now many signs and wonders were regularly done among the people by the hands of the Apostles.*[66] Yours will be unspectacular miracles, but rest assured, they will be true miracles.

Personal freedom and responsibility

29. As you go about your work, in your public life and, generally, in all temporal affairs,

---

[65] *Haec itaque cum audisset, quoniam Ozias promisisset quod transacto quinto die traderet civitatem, misit ad presbyteros Chabri et Charmi. Et venerunt ad illam, et dixit illis: quod est hoc verbum, in quo consensit Ozias, ut tradat civitatem Assyriis si intra quinque dies non venerit vobis adiutorium? Et qui estis vos, qui tentatis Dominum? Non est iste sermo, qui misericordiam provocet, sed potius qui iram excitet, et furorem accendat. Posuistis vos tempus miserationis Domini, et in arbitrium vestrum, diem constituistis ei* (Judith 8:9-13).

[66] *Per manus autem Apostolorum fiebant signa, et prodigia multa in plebe. Et erant unanimiter omnes in porticu Salomonis* (Acts 5:12):

each of you acts with personal freedom and responsibility. You form your own opinions, always in accordance with the dictates of your conscience, but with a wonderful diversity. You do not implicate – you cannot implicate – either the Church or the Work, because you have a *fully lay mentality*. Hence, you are friends of freedom and not limited by any restraints other than those indicated by the doctrine and morals of Jesus Christ.

The Work of God's purpose and the means it uses are not temporal; they are fully and exclusively supernatural and spiritual. The Work is not involved in, is foreign to, human, political and economic interests or any other such interests. It is, by its nature, transcendent to earthly society and, therefore, it can never be bound to a particular culture or tie itself to a specific era of human history. The Work has no human interests

Sometimes Opus Dei corporately promotes apostolic projects and initiatives. These projects are dedicated to education, Christian teaching, welfare and other such goals. They are known to all and open to all, including non-Catholics and non-Christians, and are carried out within the terms laid down by the civil laws of each country. These corporate works do not constitute an ecclesiastical activity, because they are quite simply professional activities of ordinary citizens, though they are apostolic at heart and in their aims. The corporate works are not ecclesiastical activities

30. But the fact that our Work is completely uninvolved in the interests of earthly society, in

Christian awareness in fulfilling civic obligations

financial or social undertakings, in political activity, and so on, does not mean that it is indifferent to the spirit or lack of spirit which inspires the institutions of the temporal city. We want citizens to be fully aware of their civic obligations and to fulfil them according to correct human criteria and with a Christian understanding of life.

Catechism of Christian Doctrine

I have often said that the Catechism of Christian Doctrine which is taught to children should include some questions and answers on these duties. In this way people would learn from childhood that these commands come from God and later, when they grow up, would feel in their conscience the responsibility to fulfil them.

A healthy anticlericalism

31. At times, the distinction our Lord made between the things that are God's and the things that are Caesar's[67] is misunderstood. Christ was distinguishing between the fields of jurisdiction of two authorities: the Church and the State. In doing so, he was forestalling the harmful effects of *Caesarism*[68] and *clericalism*. He established the doctrine of a healthy *anticlericalism*, which is a real, deep love for the priesthood: what a sorry sight it is when the exalted mission of the priest is cheapened and debased by getting mixed up in projects that are earthly and petty. He has also established the autonomy of God's Church and the legitimate

---

[67] Cf. Matt 22:21.

[68] *Caesarism:* an authoritarian or autocratic ideology.

autonomy enjoyed by civil society for the regulation and technical structuring of its affairs.

Christ's message throws light upon the whole of life

But the distinction established by Christ does not in any way mean that religion should be confined to Church affairs – to the sacristy – or that the ordering of human affairs should ignore all divine and Christian law. That would be to deny the faith of Christ, which demands adherence from the whole man, body and soul, as an individual and as a member of society.

Christ's message throws light upon the whole of human life, its foundation and its end, and not merely the narrow field of some subjective acts of piety. Laicism or secularism denies the faith which expresses itself in deeds, that faith which knows that the world's autonomy is relative, and that the ultimate meaning of everything in the world is the glory of God and the salvation of souls.

Inalienable rights of Christ

32. Therefore you will understand why the Work, like the Church, of which it is a living organ, is interested in human society: in society there are inalienable rights of Christ, which need to be protected. So much so that it can be said that all the apostolate of Opus Dei boils down to *giving doctrine*.[69] It gives doctrine so that all its members and the people who come to it for formation can carry out individually – as citizens – an apostolate of a professional nature, by sanctifying their profession,

[69] *giving doctrine*: see note to §44 below

sanctifying themselves in their profession and sanctifying others by means of their profession.

I have told you on many occasions that as a rule the Work does not act externally: it is as if it didn't exist. It is the members of the Work who, respecting the civil laws of each country, work within those laws. The activity of Opus Dei is aimed principally at giving its members thorough spiritual, doctrinal and apostolic formation.

The apostolate of the Work is a great catechesis

The apostolate of the Work is like a great catechesis, like an immense task of spiritual direction which enlightens, counsels, spurs on and sustains the conscience of many souls to prevent them from becoming bourgeois and help them to keep alive their dignity as Christians and to exercise the rights and fulfil the duties of responsible Catholic citizens.

Formation of Super-numeraries

33. My Supernumerary daughters and sons, the formation you receive in Opus Dei is flexible; it adapts to your personal and social situation like a glove to the hand. You should be very clear in your spiritual guidance, explaining the specific circumstances of your work, family, and social obligations. You should do so because, while we have only one spirit and only one set of ascetical means, these can and should become a reality in each situation without being rigid.

Speak sincerely with your Directors so that the freedom and peace of your spirit is never upset by the difficulties you encounter (oftentimes imaginary), which can always be solved. Bear in mind that the spiritual formation we receive is quite the opposite of being complicated, scrupulous, or interiorly inhibited. The spirit of the Work gives us freedom of spirit, simplifies our life, prevents us from becoming twisted and complicated. It makes us forget about ourselves, and think generously about others.

Sincerity and simplicity

Only exceptionally should you go to receive formation to the houses where the Numerary members have their family life. It is more discreet for you to see the Directors and Coordinators in your places of work, in your homes, in the street, which is the place where our Lord has called us. To receive collective formation, it is fine for you to go to one of our corporate apostolates, which have their doors and windows wide open, because they are open to all souls.

Ascetical and doctrinal formation

34. Together with ascetical formation, the Work also gives you solid doctrinal formation, which is an integral part of that common denominator – the family atmosphere – of all the children of God in Opus Dei. You need that foundation of clear ideas about fundamental issues in order to be in a position to enlighten many minds and to defend the Church from attacks, which she receives at times from all sides. You need clear ideas on dogmatic and moral truths; on the requirements of the family and Christian education; on the right to work, rest, private

Truth brings joy, peace and effectiveness

property, etc.; on the fundamental freedoms of association, expression, etc. In this way you will joyfully experience the truth of those words: *veritas liberabit vos*,[70] because the truth will bring you joy, peace and effectiveness.

In the annual workshops – which help you to keep up your initial fervour, improve your religious culture and strengthen you for the apostolate – in the Study Circles, in talks, in specialised courses and the like, you assiduously receive abundant doctrine. At the same time you are given information on topics of current interest, focused with Christian criteria. You complete this formation by reading, because you will always have libraries available for you to subscribe to, and you can encourage others who don't belong to the Work to do the same.

Make every effort to assimilate the doctrine you are taught, so that it doesn't stagnate. Feel the need and the joyful duty of bringing the formation you are receiving to other minds, so that it may result in good and upright deeds in the hearts of others too.

Dedication of the local councils for Supernumeraries

What I have said makes clear how essential it is that the local councils who look after Supernumeraries are fully dedicated to the task, because none of them – none of my children – should ever feel neglected. Careful planning will be needed to ensure they receive their formation during holiday

[70] John 8:32.

times and when they are isolated.

My children who have been entrusted with the task of governing and directing their brothers and sisters will often have to say No to a chance of personal achievement. Instead, like hidden blocks of stone, they will lay the foundation for a much more wide-ranging enterprise. They should not forget that these activities of government and formation, like that of other members who devote themselves full-time to our corporate apostolates, are also always professional work.

Complete freedom in temporal matters

35. The Work forms its members so that each of them acts, with personal freedom, in a Christian fashion in the exercise of his or her profession, in the middle of the world. In temporal affairs the Directors of the Work will never be able to impose a particular opinion. Each of you, let me repeat, behaves with complete freedom, in accordance with his or her own well-formed conscience.

Let each wayfarer follow his own path

In 1939, just after the Spanish Civil War, I preached a retreat near Valencia. It took place in a privately founded university college, which had been used during the war as a Communist barracks. In one of the corridors I found a large poster, the work of some "non-conformist", which said: "Let each wayfarer follow his own path." Some people wanted to remove it, but I held them back. "Leave it," I told them, "I like it. It is advice from the enemy."[71]

[71] *advice from the enemy*: see note to §24 above.

Especially since then, those words have often served me as a topic for preaching. Freedom: let each wayfarer follow his or her own path. It is absurd and unjust to try to impose one single criterion on everybody, in matters where the teaching of Christ does not set limits.

Cannot impose one single Christian formula in temporal matters

There should be complete freedom in all temporal affairs, because there is no one single Christian formula for ordering the things of this world. There are many technical formulas for solving social, scientific, financial and political problems, and they will all be Christian, provided they respect those minimum principles which cannot be abandoned without violating the natural law and the teaching of the Gospel.

Monopolies under the pretext of unity

There should be freedom in temporal matters, and in the Church too, my children. I am very anti-clerical, with that healthy anti-clericalism I often speak to you about, and anyone who has my spirit will be the same. Too often in clerical circles which don't have a good priestly spirit, monopolies are organised under the pretext of unity, and people try to corral souls into little groups. Pressure is put on the freedom of consciences of the faithful, who have the right to look for direction and formation for their souls wherever they judge best and with whoever they prefer. One sees a multiplication of unnecessary negative precepts, when people would be doing a lot if they just kept the commandments of God and the Church. And those who are being asked to fulfil these negative precepts end up psychologically tied into knots.

36. Freedom, my children. Don't ever expect the Work to tell you what to do in temporal affairs. Anybody who tried to violate the freedom the Work grants to its children, trampling on the rightful personality of each child of God in Opus Dei, would not have my spirit. Freedom

It is you – in all freedom – who need to develop proper sensibilities through the formation you receive. In this way you will react spontaneously to the problems of mankind, to the uncertain social circumstances that need to be given shape with upright criteria. It is up to you, along with your fellow citizens, to courageously run the risk of seeking human and Christian solutions to the temporal questions you encounter along your way. These solutions will be whatever ones you see in conscience, since there is no single solution.

You would wait in vain for the Work to give these solutions to you ready made. Such a thing hasn't ever happened, doesn't happen, nor shall it ever happen, because it is contrary to our nature. The Work is not "paternalistic", although that word is ambivalent and, therefore, I am now referring to its pejorative sense. Your Directors trust in your ability to react and take the initiative; they do not lead you by the hand. But, in the spiritual order, they do have towards you a "good paternalism": sentiments of fatherliness, and indeed of motherliness! False paternalism

We're not a pressure group

And so, precisely because of the very freedom we enjoy in Opus Dei, it is impossible for us to form within society what is nowadays called a pressure group. If ever the Directors were to formulate a particular criterion in some temporal matter, the rest of the members of the Work who think differently would legitimately rebel against it, and I would find myself with the sad duty of blessing and praising those who categorically refused to obey. They would have to bring the affair immediately to the attention of the Regional Directors, or of the Father, and reprimand with holy indignation those Directors who had tried to wield an authority which they cannot have. And it would be necessary to reprimand seriously any children of mine who, in the name of their own freedom, might attempt to limit the legitimate freedom of their brothers or sisters, by trying to impose a criterion of their own in temporal matters or matters open to various opinions.

The Directors cannot wield an authority they don't have

As for those who stubbornly refuse to see these clear things and who claim to discover signs of secrecy, a secrecy that has never existed nor will ever be needed, surely they do so *ex abundantia cordis,* because that is how they themselves behave. And they will never walk as we do, with their heads up and looking others straight in the eye, because we don't have anything to hide, even though everyone has failings which he fights against in his interior life.

37. It has happened, over these thirty one years, that some people out of jealousy have looked unkindly upon our work. Others have not been very sympathetic, because they do not like the Church, which we serve for the good of all mankind. There have even been some (fortunately not all that many), whose clerical mentality makes them incapable of understanding the essentially lay nature of the work my children do. Others do not realise or do not want to remember that God our Lord grants his grace – specific grace – to the souls who follow him. And so, in order to explain the intensity, the extension and the effectiveness of the apostolates of the Work, they invent human causes, totally false, given that the Work's ends are supernatural and the means we use are also exclusively spiritual and supernatural: prayer, sacrifice and work that is sanctified and sanctifying.

People who do not understand our work

There are people who are unable to respect and understand the personal freedom of others, so much so that they seem impermeable to the truth that the members of Opus Dei have a common objective, which is exclusively spiritual in nature, and is the only thing on which they speak with one voice; that they are free citizens in temporal affairs, just like the rest of the laity, their fellow-citizens; and that they ought to live peaceably with everybody.

The purpose of the Work is exclusively spiritual

Some of these people, as I said, come from the closed atmosphere of the sacristy, and are used to seeing how the religious habitually express their opinions in accordance with *the school of their own religious family* or in accordance with *their Superiors' way of thinking*. Consequently, *with that prejudiced clerical mentality*, they have wanted to apply a sort of label to Opus Dei or to me personally, calling me a monarchist or a republican – or even a freemason – simply because I have not excluded any soul from our activity as children of God.

Associations of the faithful

38. Your apostolic work, my children, is not an ecclesiastical activity.[72] And although there is nothing wrong in itself with some of you belonging to associations of the faithful, that will not be the norm, because the specific apostolate that the Work prepares you for – the work that God wants of us – is not of a denominational kind.

With this discretion of ours we practise a

---

[72] *Your apostolic work, my children, is not an ecclesiastical activity*: that is, for St Josemaría the apostolate is the task of each person, not of the institution, which limits itself to orienting and assisting pastorally the people who belong to or come to Opus Dei. His idea is that apostolic action is always the responsibility and fruit of the initiative of the members, Cooperators or friends, who benefit from the guidance and spiritual help given to them.
is not of a denominational kind: the mission, as disciples of Jesus in the world, springs from the baptismal awareness and unfolds in the personal relationships that each one nurtures. Therefore, using a paradox, he says that a profoundly Christian apostolate such as the one he is describing, may not have an officially Catholic or "confessional" nuance, since it is presented as something that comes from one's own intimate life of faith, in the exercise of one's own secular profession or activity.

wonderful collective humility. By working silently, without making a show of successes or triumphs – but, let me insist, without any sort of mystery or secrecy, which we don't need in order to serve God – you pass unnoticed among the other Catholic faithful (you are just that: Catholic faithful), without getting applause for the good seed you sow.

Collective humility

All the same, especially in rural areas, where it might appear odd to do otherwise, some of you can be involved in confraternities and other parish apostolic activities, trying to encourage them and to give them life, but ordinarily not taking leadership roles in them. Consequently, those people running associations of the faithful who – unfortunately – may like to monopolise things, will have no reason to worry that we will snatch their exclusivist dictatorship from them, because our idea is that they are the ones to run these activities. We should act in our own way, which is quite different.

Taking part in public acts of worship

But, like the Christian faithful you are, unless the circumstances and the greater effectiveness of the apostolate suggest otherwise, you shouldn't be absent from public acts of worship, which society as such has a duty to render to God. I have suffered so often on seeing public acts of worship from which the community was absent: one didn't see there God's family, his people. I am sure that, if you are faithful, acts of public worship will be genuine, sober and dignified, without the fussy or exaggerated trappings which so often give them the appearance of a show.

Apostolate in the exercise of civic duties and rights

39. Let me remind you once again, my children, that the specific apostolate you are called to carry out is to be done by you as citizens, with full and sincere fidelity to the State, in keeping with the gospel and apostolic teaching.[73] You should comply faithfully with the law of the land and fulfil all your civic duties, without trying to escape any obligation and exercising all your rights, for the good of society, without imprudently opting out of any of them.

Concerning the exercise of citizens' rights, we find a living example in the repeated behaviour of St Paul, as described in the Acts of the Apostles. His is a manly firmness, which the timid could perceive as arrogance. Really, it is upright honesty with no nonsense. When necessary, the Apostle declares his status as a Roman citizen and he demands, without any false humility, to be treated as such: *They have beaten us publicly, uncondemned, men who are Roman citizens, and have thrown us into prison; and do they now cast us out secretly? No! Let them* (the ministers of justice) *come themselves and take us out*.[74]

The example of St Paul

How forthright Paul is with the jailer at Philippi! And there is his wonderful conversation with the tribune in Jerusalem, full of human elegance, when he is on the point of being

---

[73] Cf. Matt 22:15-22; Mark 12:13-17; Luke 20:20-26; Rom 13:1-7.

[74] Acts 16:37.

scourged: *But when they had strapped him down, Paul said to the centurion who was standing by, "Is it lawful for you to scourge a man who is a Roman citizen and uncondemned?" When the centurion heard that, he went to the tribune and said to him, "What are you about to do? For this man is a Roman citizen." So the tribune came and said to him, "Tell me, are you a Roman citizen?" And he said, "Yes." The tribune answered, "I bought this citizenship for a large sum." Paul said, "But I was born a citizen."*[75] There is no need for comment, my daughters and sons: learn the lesson.

State intrusion in the private sphere

40. From time to time I have pointed out to you the regrettable fact of the State's progressive invasion into the private sphere, with the corresponding servitude this entails for citizens as it deprives them of their lawful rights. And I have underlined that the State is cold and without feeling, so that its totalitarianism turns into something worse than the harshest situations of feudalism.

Leaving aside other considerations, if this kind of thing happens, it is, to a great extent, due to the citizens' own failure to act, to their passivity in defending the sacred rights of the human person. This inactivity, which has its origin in mental laziness and lack of motivation, is also to be found among Catholic citizens, who do not seem to be aware that there are other sins – and graver ones – than those against the Sixth Commandment.

---

[75] Acts 22:25-28; cf. Acts 25:11.

No human task can be a matter of indifference to us

41. My daughters and sons, from the mission that God has entrusted to us and from the fully secular character of our vocation it can be deduced that no event, no human task can be a matter of indifference to us. For this reason I stress that you must be present in the social activities that spring from human relations or influence those relations directly or indirectly. You have to give a truly Christian spirit to your colleagues at work, to associations of parents and large families, trade unions, the press, and to artistic, literary and sporting associations and competitions, etc.

Each of you will take part in such public activities in accordance with your own social condition and in the way best suited to your personal circumstances. You will do so, of course, with total freedom, both when you are acting individually and when you are working together with whatever groups of citizens you see fit to join.

Taking part in public life

You understand very well that the participation in public life I am talking about is not political activity in the strict sense of the word. Very few of my children work *professionally*, so to speak, in politics. What I am talking about is the participation proper to all citizens who are conscious of their civic duties. You should feel impelled to act – with personal freedom and responsibility – for all the same noble reasons that move your fellow citizens. But as well as that, you feel especially urged on by your apostolic zeal and the desire to carry out an apostolate of peace and understanding in all human activities.

42. When you work like this, united to your fellow countrymen and giving them courage, creating an atmosphere so that things are not imposed without allowing the legitimate feelings of society to be expressed, you will be able to give a Christian orientation to the legislation of your national communities, above all in those key issues for the public life of nations: laws on marriage, education, public morality, property, etc.

Giving a Christian orientation to legislation

How can legislation be Christian if respect for the family is based on divorce? Where is the logic when some societies which pride themselves on their religious "diversity" do not permit that diversity in state schools, where every student should have the right to receive religious education in conformity with his or her faith?

Don't you realise that private property (within the limits demanded by the common good) is an instrument for man's freedom, a good that should be seen as one of the fundamental goods required for the development of the human person and the family? Countries where these rights are not respected are not Catholic countries or even human. Do you see the panorama before you? In these and in other points of capital importance you must fight, and fight hard!

43. Work actively with our Cooperators.

Work with Cooperators

Increase their number, without fear: the more the better. Look after them, form them; they should always have a job in hand, something to do. Keep them moving, as in doing sport. Constantly broaden the base of your circle of friends and provide them, one way or another, with doctrine and encouragement. That way you will spread further the divine net which, while it may be weak, is effective. And if you keep up the vigour of this good apostolic spirit you will do an incalculable amount of good, gently and powerfully, to the whole of humanity.

Spiritual help from religious communities

We will also be helped by the prayer and hidden life of religious communities (especially enclosed orders) whom we admit as Cooperators and who understand very well our contemplative spirit in the middle of the world. They are contemplatives from their place apart from the world; we are contemplatives in the bosom and structures of civil society. Two expressions – different and specifically distinct – of the same love for Jesus Christ.

Among us there are very many friends and Cooperators, who work nobly shoulder to shoulder with us in apostolic tasks or lend a hand so that we can work. Some are quite distant from God our Lord or do not know him. Meditate on those words of St Peter: *satagite ut, per bona opera, certam vestram vocationem et electionem faciatis.*[76] Strive so that

[76] 2 Pet 1:10 (Vg): "Strive, brethren, even more by good works, to make your calling and election sure." The Neo-vulgate

these friends of ours, whom we love like brothers, continue their good works. Never doubt that, if we help them with our prayer and loyal friendship – always with the greatest respect for personal freedom – many of them will receive the grace to choose to become Christians.

44. Don't forget that the essence of our apostolate is to give doctrine,[77] because, as I have told you a thousand times, ignorance is the greatest enemy of the faith. St Paul wrote to the Romans: *How then will they call upon him in whom they have not believed? And how are they to believe in him of whom they have never heard? And how are they to hear without someone preaching?*[78] Because you feel this responsibility to preach, you give great importance to the task of teaching – private or public; personal or collective; at primary, secondary or higher level – even though teaching is a small part of our professional work.

Spreading doctrine

Teaching in both private and public schools

For the same reason, you try to infuse life into the institutions that shape public opinion: the

The media

---

version has changed the text of the Vulgate which St Josemaría quotes here, eliminating "*per bona opera*" ("by good works").

[77] *to give doctrine*: St Josemaría often uses this expression as a synonym for expounding the Christian truth, the deposit of faith, in the most varied contexts and forms; or, in other words, to spread the Gospel message through one's personal and professional activity. It does not necessarily refer to a catechetical activity, since it also includes the first proclamation to those who do not believe in Christ.

[78] Rom 10:14.

press, radio, television, films, and so on. Those of you who are professionally involved in these areas do not just teach doctrine to a small group of people, as in a Circle or a lecture, but, like our Lord, you preach to the multitude, in *the open air*.

Religious ignorance is rampant all around us and we Christians can take much of the blame. We fail to teach doctrine through all these means of communication, which are daily becoming more advanced technologically and more influential and which are so often controlled by the enemies of God.

Proclaiming the truth untiringly

45. The worst thing in the world, my children, is that people do horrendous things and don't realise that they are doing them. Proclaim the truth untiringly – *opportune, importune*[79] – even though some do not believe us or do not want to believe us. *Quidquid recipitur ad modum recipientis recipitur*:[80] that is why they don't believe us. We can give them the wine of the marriage-feast at Cana, which was witness to Jesus' first miracle, the first public manifestation of his divinity. Yet, on being poured into the minds of these people, it will turn into vinegar. Still, let us continue pouring out good wine, speaking the truth! Like Jesus, each one of us – *ipse Christus* – should be able to say, *for this purpose I*

[79] 2 Tim 4:2: "in season and out of season".

[80] *Quidquid recipitur ad modum recipientis recipitur*: "Whatever is received, is received according to the capacity of the receiver" is a typically scholastic philosophical aphorism. The concept is used, for example, by St Thomas Aquinas.

have come into the world, to bear witness to the truth.[81]

My children, *having put away falsehood, let each one of you speak the truth with his neighbour; for we are members of one another.*[82] We know something of the pain of being spoken badly of, lied about and slandered. Here the *we* is very appropriate, for we have felt it in our very flesh. We have felt great waves of filth, sometimes provoked by Catholics and even priests. *Omnia in bonum!* Just as the Nile, after bursting its banks, would fertilise the fields with its silt when it receded; so too with us, those waves of filth have filled us with fruitfulness.

Get-togethers periodically with friends and colleagues

46. Organise little get-togethers periodically with your friends and colleagues, and particularly with media professionals. In them bring up topical issues and, give sound ideas with the gift of tongues. Try also to strike up conversations opportunely in offices and public places.

Don't miss opportunities – create them – to speak the truth and sow good seed. *Walk in wisdom towards outsiders, making the best use of the time. Let your speech always be gracious, seasoned with salt, so that you may know how you ought to answer each person.*[83]

---

[81] *Dixit itaque ei Pilatus: ergo rex es tu? Respondit Iesus: tu dicis quia rex sum ego. Ego in hoc natus sum, et ad hoc veni in mundum, ut testimonium perhibeam veritati: omnis qui est ex veritate, audit vocem meam* (John 18:37).

[82] *Propter quod deponentes mendacium, loquimini veritatem unusquisque cum proximo suo, quoniam sumus invicem membra* (Eph 4:25).

[83] Col 4:5-6.

Workers connected with the press

With great hope I think of those children of mine who run newspaper stalls and shops, and of those who work in publishing, in newsrooms and in companies doing graphic design; and of those others who, through their work, however modest it may seem, have the opportunity every day of engaging with lots of people.

Entertainment apostolate

47. Parents, try to foster healthy and cheerful entertainments, which steer clear equally from being prim and prudish and from a worldly tone which offends Christian morality. From those gatherings, there will result – our Lord will bless them – marriages among your children, who will inherit the happiness and peace that they have learnt in your *bright and cheerful* homes.

In the field of this entertainment apostolate, don't forget that the absolutely key point which you have to defend with your action as citizens is the morality of public spectacles. It is difficult for young people who live in a generalised environment of easy immorality to go on to form Christian homes.

The sphere of finance is also a field for our apostolic work

48. It would be a sign of deformation if we ever thought that the sphere of economics and finance cannot be a field for our apostolic work. This notion is widespread among people who come from clerical circles. Yet it is accompanied with the paradox that many of these same people – under the Church's wing – are often involved in companies and business dealings and handle large sums of money from other people who trust them because they *call themselves* Catholic. It has been said of such men, not too maliciously, that their eyes are in heaven and their hands on whatever they can get hold of. To have reservations and prejudices about financial affairs is not a Christian attitude, because this is just one more task that is to be sanctified.

Nevertheless, this suspicion on the part of Catholics has had, and still has, a lot of influence, and has often held them back from doing good with their work in this field of finance. Sometimes they have worked there but with a guilty conscience or they have left these human tasks to the power of people hostile to the Church, who have been able and continue to be able to use them to do a great deal of harm to souls.

All honest jobs can be orientated with a Christian and apostolic spirit

So much is this the case that it is amusing to read certain pious considerations from ecclesiastical tradition (justified no doubt by the mentality and atmosphere of the times) stating that after our Lord's resurrection Peter could go back to his job as a fisherman because fishing is an honest job, but it was not lawful for Matthew to go back to his profession. This would be because there are jobs which it is impossible to do without a grave risk of sin or, put simply and crudely, without committing sin. And Matthew's was one of these.[84]

[84] *Nam piscatorem Petrum, Matthaeum vero telonearium scimus; et post conversionem suam ad piscationem Petrus rediit, Matthaeus vero*

We have to put an end to such mistaken concepts, created by people who profess the *contemptus saeculi*, contempt for the world. Your lay mentality sees nothing wrong in the fact of working in business or finance, because you know how to supernaturalise those tasks, like all the others you do, and orient them with a Christian and apostolic spirit.

49. And while we are on the subject, I want to tell you that, unfortunately, what people say about our activities in the world of finance is not true. Actually they are almost non-existent: the normal ones for keeping alive and raising a large, poor family. Would that they were a thousand times greater than they are!

The Work is poor and always will be: it has many needs to support

All organisations, of whatever kind, have to manage funds to carry out their aims. It's a pity that the people who gossip about us this way are not right! Even if they were right, the Work would

---

ad telonei negotium non resedit: quia aliud est victum per piscationem quaerere, aliud autem telonei lucris pecunias augere. Sunt enim pleraque negotia, quae sine peccatis exhiberi aut vix aut nullatenus possunt. Quae ergo ad peccatum implicant, ad haec necesse est ut post conversionem animus non recurrat (St Gregory the Great, *Homilies on the Gospels*, 24): "For we know that Peter was a fisherman, but Matthew a tax collector; and after his conversion Peter returned to his fishing. But Matthew did not go back to his tax collecting bench: because one thing is to seek one's living by fishing, another to increase one's income by tax collecting earnings. For there are a good many jobs which can scarcely or not at all be done without sin. To those therefore that lead to sin it is necessary that one should not be minded to return after conversion."

still be poor, as it always will be. The Work has to support many apostolic undertakings all over the world, which run at a loss; it has to form its members, throughout their life, and that costs money; it has to look after its sick and elderly members; and we will always have the blessed burden, which increases daily, of giving financial support to the parents of members of the Work, if they are old or sick, or need help to keep going, etc.

In any case, those financial activities, if they exist – and they should come to exist as soon as possible – will always be done by us in accordance with the laws of the land, paying rates and taxes, as the most honest citizen does. We do not want, it's *not our style*, to live off privileges.

50. Sometimes the people who criticise us belong to some official group, which lives off tax-payers' money against the wishes of that country's citizens. At the same time they would like us to have no room to breathe, no right to work or sacrifice ourselves as we do, living in poverty so as to maintain and carry out works of charity, education, culture and promotion of Christian doctrine. They are enemies of freedom – that is, of other people's freedom – and they want to practise discrimination among citizens.

All associations, of whatever kind, religious, artistic, sporting, cultural, and so on, must necessarily own and manage money in order to maintain the instruments they need to use in fulfilling their aims. Anyone who is scandalised by this shows a great lack of common sense, to say the least.

When I mention religious associations, there come to mind immediately the Bible Society,[85] or the Salvation Army which have a bank, an insurance company and so on. Nobody is scandalised. They need those means in order to spread their message and maintain their welfare work. In many countries, not only are these religious associations not criticised for their financial activities but the State exempts them from taxes, because of the social work they do.

It is perfectly just, therefore, for official bodies anywhere in the world to make us loans and even donations. Should they do so, they will be doing no more than fulfilling their duty, because through our public and social work we are lifting part of their obligations off their shoulders. If these authorities help us in the same way as they help other cultural and charitable institutions, they will be doing no more than what is just.

Work is a means of sanctification and apostolate

51. Opus Dei, *operatio Dei,* God's work, requires all its members to work, because work is a means of sanctification and apostolate. That is why

[85] *the Bible Society*: originally called The British and Foreign Bible Society, or simply The Bible Society, was founded in 1804 at the London Tavern. With other Bible societies, it is part of the United Bible Societies, which tries to make the Bible accessible worldwide. *Salvation Army*: The Salvation Army is a Protestant Christian denomination and charity, founded in 1865.

so many millions of people all over the world, Catholics and non-Catholics, Christians and non-Christians, admire and love and help our Work with deep affection. And we thank God for it.

There are also some among you who, because they feel they have the qualifications to take an active part in solving the public problems of their country, are involved in political life, with full freedom and personal responsibility. You are not many: the normal percentage as in society at large. And like all the other members of the Work in their earthly occupations, when you work in this field you always do so without presenting yourselves as Catholics or members of the Work as a way to get ahead. You do not make use of the Church or the Work, because you know that you cannot mix either God's Church or the Work with temporal affairs. Moreover, when you are working in public life, you cannot forget that what we Catholics desire is a society of free citizens, all having the same duties and the same rights with regard to the State, but united in and agreeing on an effective work to attain the common good by applying the principles of the Gospel, which are the constant source of the Church's teaching.

The right to follow a vocation to be a politician

You have every right to follow the vocation of a politician. Were any State to put obstacles in your way, it would have to put the same obstacles in the way of the members of other associations of the faithful. And then, for the same reason, namely, the obedience that the faithful owe to the ecclesiastical authorities, the State (being logically consistent) would place the same impediments on all practising Catholics, denying them their full rights and responsibilities in temporal society. It is unjust to treat practising Catholics as inferior citizens, but one comes across examples of this kind of discrimination in contemporary history.

With the aim of serving others

To those of you who have a vocation for politics I say: work fearlessly and realise that, if you do not do so, you would be sinning by omission. Work with professional endeavour and fulfil the technical demands of your job. Aim to offer a Christian service to everyone in your country, and keep concord among all nations in mind.

A symptom of clerical mentality is found in the praises, written by people who have withdrawn from the world, which the liturgy makes of rulers who have been canonised. They are lauded more for having ruled their kingdoms with piety than with the exercise of their royal power, *pietate magis quam imperio*, more with kindness rather than with authority.

Do not mix the divine with the human

In fulfilling your mission, do so with a pure intention, without losing your supernatural outlook, but do not mix the divine with the human. Do things as human beings should do them, and don't forget that the orders of creation have their own principles and laws, which must not be violated by drawing false comparisons with angels. The worst praise that I can pay to a son of mine is to say that he is like an angel. We are not angels, we are human beings.

Presence of Catholics in the government of nations

52. Those of you who work in public life should feel it your duty not to abstain from that work under any regime, even those which are not guided by Christian principles, unless the local Church hierarchy establishes otherwise for Catholics. Your conscience does not permit you to leave government affairs to those who are not Catholics, and even in circumstances which are most hostile to religion you will always be able to prevent greater evils from being done.

Regardless of the system of government, you should not abandon the field,[86] even though people

[86] *Regardless of the system of government, you should not abandon the field*: the option proposed by St Josemaría is to work in this sector by following one's professional vocation. Unless the Catholic hierarchy orders otherwise, as happened, for example, in Italy between 1868 and 1919, with the *non expedit* (it does not suit), which forbade Catholics to participate actively or passively in political elections, in protest against the anti-Catholic laws of the Kingdom of Italy. In the case of Opus Dei, the accusation of collaboration with General Franco's regime is well known, since two of its members entered the Spanish government in 1957 and others did so in successive years. However, the Spanish Catholic hierarchy did not discourage, but rather supported, the collaboration of Catholics with the Franco regime, which, although it did not recognise political freedoms, seemed to guarantee the presence of the evangelical message in public life. For this reason, St Josemaría respected the choice of those members of Opus Dei who supported Franco, as well as those in the Work who opposed the dictator. Curiously, both options ended up

might – unjustly – label you as a collaborator. My children, all this is even more important in countries with a Catholic majority. It would be incomprehensible if in the Government there were no practising and responsible Catholics and, therefore, no members of the various associations of the faithful. Otherwise we would have to say that the Catholics in that country are neither practising nor responsible nor Catholic, or that the Church is being persecuted.

Effort to promulgate just laws

Should you have to take part in the work of government, do all you can to promulgate just laws that the citizens can fulfil. To do the contrary is an abuse of power and an assault on people's freedom. Besides, it deforms their consciences, because in such cases they have a perfect right not to comply with those laws which are laws in name only.

Respect for the freedom of all

Respect the freedom of all citizens, and bear in mind that all the members of the community should participate in the common good. Give everyone the opportunity to raise their standard of living, without pushing down some people in order to lift up the rest. Offer the humbler folk open horizons for their future: job security and proper pay, access to equal education. Besides being what is right and just, this will bring light to their lives, change their attitudes and help them to

---

damaging, in one way or another, the image of Opus Dei, but the founder did not change his criterion, thus maintaining the total freedom of the members in political matters.

search for God and the higher realities. However, do not forget, my dear children, that the saddest poverty is spiritual poverty, being deprived of Christ's doctrine and not partaking in his life.

53. My Supernumerary daughters and sons, I am thinking now about your homes, your families, which have grown out of the *sacramentum magnum*[87] of marriage. At a time when the destructive work done against the family in the past century still continues, we have come to bring the desire for holiness to this Christian cell of society.

The first apostolate of Supernumeraries is in their home

Your first apostolate is in the home. The formation that Opus Dei gives you leads you to appreciate the beauty of the family, the supernatural work entailed in forming a home and the fount of sanctification that lies hidden in your conjugal duties. At the same time as being aware of the greatness of your vocation to marriage – it's that, a vocation! – you experience a special veneration and deep affection for the perfect chastity which you know is higher than marriage.[88] Consequently, you are truly happy when, by

---

[87] Cf. Eph 5:32.

[88] Cf. Matt 19:11 ff., 1 Cor 7:25-40. *Si quis dixerit, statum coniugalem anteponendum esse statui virginitatis vel coelibatus, et non esse melius ac beatius, manere in virginitate aut coelibatu, quam iungi matrimonio: A.S.* "If any one says that the married state is to be placed above the state of virginity or celibacy, and that it is not better and more blessed to remain in virginity or in celibacy than to be united in matrimony, let him be anathema" (Council of Trent, session 24, canon 10). See also note to §10.

God's grace, one of your children embraces that other path, which *is not a sacrifice* but rather a choice made through God's goodness, a reason for holy pride, a way of joyfully serving everyone out of love for Jesus Christ.

Dignity and wholesomeness of marriage

Normally in schools, even though they are run by religious, young people are not formed to appreciate the dignity and wholesomeness of marriage. You are not unaware of this. It often happens that in the retreats – that are customarily given to pupils in the final years of secondary school – the students are offered more advice for considering a possible religious vocation than for orienting them to marriage. Indeed, there are some teachers who speak to the young people so disparagingly of marriage that it can seem to them as to be something that the Church merely tolerates.

Marriage is a divine path on earth

In Opus Dei we have always acted differently. While making it very clear that perfect chastity is superior to the married state, we have highlighted marriage as a divine path on earth. Following this way hasn't turned out badly, because the truth is always liberating, and young hearts are very generous in soaring above the flesh when they are given the freedom to choose Love.

The holy Sacrament of marriage

As for us, we are not afraid of human love, that holy love of our parents which our Lord used to give us life. I bless this love with both my hands. I won't allow any of my children not to have a great love for the holy Sacrament of marriage. And so, we are not afraid to sing the songs of wholesome human love, which are also *songs of human love in a divine key*.[89] And we who have renounced this earthly love, for Love, are not bachelors or old maids: our hearts are soft and tender.

54. My daughters and sons, I ask all of you whom God has called to form a family, to love each other dearly, to have always the same sense of romance as when you were dating. It would be a poor idea of marriage, which is an ideal and a vocation, to think that the happiness ends when the hardships and setbacks of life begin.

An ideal and a vocation

It is then that love is strengthened, and becomes stronger than death: *fortis est ut mors dilectio*.[90] Torrents of hardships and difficulties cannot quench true love: sacrifice generously shared unites you more deeply – *aquae multae non potuerunt extinguere caritatem*[91] – and the many difficulties that come, whether physical or moral, will not be able to extinguish your affection.

Your marriage, ordinarily, will be very fruitful. And if God doesn't grant you children, you will dedicate your energies more intensely to the

Receive children with joy

---

[89] *songs of human love in a divine key*: this is an implicit reference to the poetic work of St John of the Cross (1542-1591), who wrote some of his immortal poems "*in a divine key*", that is, with spiritual meaning, in everything similar to the human love couplets of other Renaissance authors.

[90] Song 8:6: "love is strong as death".

[91] Song 8:7: "many waters cannot quench love".

apostolate, which will bring you a splendid spiritual fruitfulness. As I've told you many times, the Lord usually crowns Christian families with a crown of children. Always receive them with joy and gratitude, because they are a gift and blessing from God and a proof of his confidence in you.

Do not block the sources of life

55. In the same way as the human mind is like a spark of light from the divine intellect, so the power to bring children into the world is like a participation in the creative power of God. Do not block the sources of life! Do not be afraid! Those theories (neither Christian nor human) that try to justify the need to limit births with false financial, social or scientific reasons are criminal, and, when you analyse them, they do not hold up. They are cowardice, my children – cowardice and a wish to justify the unjustifiable.

It is regrettable that these ideas often come from casuistic arguments posed by priests and religious. They meddle imprudently in matters where nobody asked them to get involved, and reveal at times a morbid curiosity. They also show that they have little love for the Church – among other things – because the Lord chose to establish the sacrament of marriage as a means for the growth and spread of his Mystical Body.

Vocations who dedicate their whole lives to God in large families

Do not doubt it: a decrease in the number of children in Christian families would bring with it a decrease in the number of vocations to the priesthood and of souls who want to dedicate their whole lives to the service of Jesus Christ. I have seen quite a few cases of married couples who, having been given only one child by God, have had the generosity to offer that child to God. But there are not many who act that way. In large families it is easier to understand the greatness of the divine vocation and, among their children, there are some for all states and walks of life.

56. For your part be generous and experience the happiness and strength of a large family. As for couples who don't want to have children, to shame them I say: "If you don't want to have children, be continent!" I think, and I say so sincerely, that it is not Christian to recommend[92] that couples should

Generosity

[92] *it is not Christian to recommend*: St Josemaría is proposing a very high ideal of marital vocation, a call to heroic holiness, in the midst of an increasingly permissive climate, which was spreading in western society of the 1960's. One senses his concern that periodic continence should not be understood as if it were a "Catholic" method of contraception, of general application, detached from the medical, human and spiritual aspects that such a choice entails for each individual. That is why he will say, in the next paragraph, that in specific cases *it can and should even be permitted*, but he will recommend that advice be sought from a doctor and a priest. He wishes to help those who seek to live their marriage in a Christian and holy way, and who, at the same time, need to distance births. In general, his words follow the pastoral orientation and Catholic moral praxis in force between 1959 and 1966, the dates when the *Letter* is dated and printed. This doctrine was clarified and perfected shortly afterwards by St Paul VI's 1968 encyclical *Humanae vitae*. The encyclical alludes to the "serious reasons" that must be given for using natural methods if births are to be spaced out (cf. no. 16). At the same time, the encyclical explains, these methods cannot be

abstain during the periods when nature has given the woman the capacity of procreating.

In some specific cases, and always with the agreement of the doctor and the priest, it can and even should be permitted. But this practice cannot be recommended as a general rule. I have told you, with very strong words,[93] that many of us would

---

separated from "responsible parenthood" and the virtue of chastity. In the period when this *Letter* of St Josemaría came out, there was a theological debate on the question and the Magisterium itself was still clarifying its position, along the lines already indicated in 1965 by the Second Vatican Council's *Gaudium et spes* (nos. 50-51). The current *Catechism of the Catholic Church* (nos. 2369-2370) takes up the formulation of *Humanae vitae*, enriched by the Magisterium of St John Paul II.

[93] *with very strong words*: let us recall that St Josemaría was writing for those who knew well his way of speaking, frank and unabashed. At the same time, he often used hyperbole in his preaching and writings to underline a teaching, as when he said that he believed his children more than a thousand unanimous notaries, or that he would rather cut his tongue with his teeth and spit it out and so many other examples of great expressive effectiveness. Hyperbolic ways of speaking, which he clearly did not intend to be taken literally. Anyone familiar with St Josemaría's love for his parents and his capacity for forgiveness and his understanding of human weaknesses, which is evident in his writings, and so evident in this *Letter*, could deduce that he would never do what he says here. But he wants to use *very strong words* to sensitise his readers to the drama experienced by those who discover they are unwanted children. This is a serious existential and psychological problem, which is especially acute in our society, following the enormous spread of contraceptive methods and abortive practices, as a result of the so-called sexual revolution, which was already on the doorstep when St Josemaría wrote these words. He wishes to make it clear that the model of holiness he

go and spit on the tombs of our parents, if we knew that we had come into the world against their will, that we hadn't been the fruit of their chaste love. Fortunately, we generally have to thank the Lord for having been born into a Christian family, to which, in large part, we owe our vocation.

Growth of the People of God

I remember a son of mine, who was working in a country where theories about birth control were very widespread. A person asked him about the matter, and he responded jokingly: "That way in a short time the only ones left in the world will be blacks and Catholics."[94] But this is not understood

proposes for married people includes a *clean love* between spouses and a great love for children, without fear – except for grave reasons – of the offspring that God wants to send.

94 *the only ones left in the world will be blacks and Catholics*: a phrase that must be understood in the historical context of the demand for civil rights in the United States in the 1950s and 1960s, when this *Letter* was written. Those years coincided with the spread of birth control measures in America, which for African-American activists concealed a racist purpose. Catholics also opposed such measures, albeit on moral grounds. The ironic phrase quoted by St Josemaría is meant to mock the racist and anti-Papist prejudices often shared by some sectors of the population, who deplored the higher birth rate of African-Americans and Catholics. St Josemaría takes the opportunity to ridicule these prejudices, jocularly quoting the irony of this member of the Work, which shows – by reduction to absurdity – the senselessness of racism and of all discrimination on religious grounds.

In 1972, an African-American asked St Josemaría how to improve his apostolate with his race (the transcript reads that the young man said 'apostolate with the blacks', a word which in Spanish did not have the pejorative meaning it now has in other languages). We have the words that St Josemaría replied:

by Catholics in countries where they are in a minority, because they don't fully comprehend the fact – which has a deep theological foundation – that in God's ordinary providence, Christian marriage is the means given for making the People of God grow.

By contrast, Christ's enemies (who are more clever) show more common sense. In countries under Communist rule, more and more importance is being given to the laws governing life and to man's creative energies, and they insert these into their ideological and political plans as decisive factors.

Bright and cheerful homes

57. In your homes, which I have always called bright and cheerful, your children will be educated in the supernatural and human virtues, in an atmosphere of freedom and cheerful sacrifice. And many, many vocations will come to the Work, from those homes which I have called the "apostolic schools" of Opus Dei! One of the great and frequent joys of my life is to see a face that reminds me of someone I knew many years ago. "What's your name?" I ask. "Are you the son of so-and-so?" And I rejoice, giving thanks to God, when he says Yes, he is.

Happiness in everyday things

The secret of married happiness lies in everyday things: in discovering hidden joys when you

---

Look, my son, before God there are neither blacks nor whites: we are all equal, all equal! I love you with all my soul, just as I love this one and that one, and everyone. We must overcome the barrier of race, because there is no barrier: we are all the same colour: the colour of the children of God (notes of a meeting, 3 April 1972).

come home; in bringing up the children; in work in which the whole family cooperates; also in making good use of all the advances that progress has provided, to make the home more pleasant, formation more effective and life simpler (with nothing that smacks of a convent, as that would be abnormal).

Gratitude of families for the vocation of their children

58. You can also help by reaching out to those other (few) families of some of my children, who are finding it hard to understand their children's dedication to God's service. You will help them to be grateful to God for the inestimable favour of having been called to be fathers and mothers of children of God in his Work. It never occurred to them that their children would dedicate themselves to God, but rather they had made very different plans for them. They had not foreseen this dedication and it came along and shattered their noble but earthly projects. In any case, my long experience has taught me that parents who do not at first joyfully accept their child's vocation eventually come around; they draw closer to a life of piety, to the Church, and end up loving the Work.

In spite of what I have just said, every day there are, thank God, more and more families – parents, brothers and sisters, relatives – who react to a vocation in a supernatural and Christian way. They lend us a hand, they ask to join the Work as Supernumeraries, or at least they are great Cooperators.

When I speak with the mothers and fathers of my children, I often tell them: "Your mission as parents hasn't finished. You have to help them to be saints. How? By being saints yourselves. You are fulfilling a duty of parenthood by helping them, helping me, to be holy. Let me tell you something: Opus Dei's pride and joy, its crown, are you mothers and fathers who have a piece of your heart dedicated to the service of the Church."

59. I'm finishing now, my beloved daughters and sons. *I have written to you somewhat freely, to refresh your memory,*[95] although I well know your desire to be faithful to our Lord's call.

Fulfilling our mission with daring

Fulfil your mission daringly and don't be afraid to commit yourselves, to stand up for what is right, because people are easily scared of exercising their freedom. They prefer to be given ready-made formulas for everything. It is a paradox, but people often ask for a rule, and renounce their freedom, for fear of taking a risk.

The Work forms you so that each of you, in your own surroundings, may bravely be a man or woman of initiative, drive and leadership. You should respond to this formation with determination and energy. Without that decisiveness on your part, all these spiritual resources would go for nothing. Recall the phrase which was often engraved on ancient daggers: "Do not rely on me

---

[95] *Audacius autem scripsi vobis, fratres, ex parte tanquam in memoriam vos reducens: propter gratiam, quae data est mihi a Deo* (Rom 15:15): "I have written to you very boldly by way of reminder, because of the grace given me by God."

if you lack a stout heart."

Resolute, tenacious and persevering

Be resolute, tenacious and persevering, *and never take "No" for an answer*. Be understanding towards everyone, aiming especially for unity among Catholics. *If you bite and devour one another, watch out that you are not consumed by one another,*[96] said St Paul. We Catholics, therefore, need to know and love one another.

Christian austerity and sacrifice

60. Give to everyone the example of your Christian austerity and your sacrifice. Our Lord has told us: *If any one would come after me, let him deny himself.*[97] He, my children, has made us experience the fruitfulness of seeing ourselves trampled on, crushed in the winepress, like grapes, in order to become… Christ's wine!

Divine filiation

At all times be serene, neither violent nor aggressive nor hot-headed, with that serenity which requires the practice of the cardinal virtues. A vivid awareness of our divine filiation will give you that serenity, because this characteristic feature of our spirit was born with the Work, and in 1931 it took shape.[98] In humanly difficult moments, in which I had nevertheless the certainty of the impossible (what you contemplate today as a reality) I felt the Lord's action, bringing forth in my heart and to

---

[96] *Quod si invicem mordetis, et comeditis: videte ne ab invicem consumamini* (Gal 5:15).

[97] Matt 16:24.

[98] *in 1931 it took shape*: the fact was recalled several times by the founder of Opus Dei, who considered it an important light from God.

my lips, with the force of something imperiously Abba! Pater! necessary, this tender invocation: *Abba! Pater!* I was in the street, on a tram. The street doesn't hinder our contemplative dialogue, because the hubbub of the world is, for us, a place for prayer. Probably I said that prayer aloud, and people must have thought I was mad: *Abba! Pater!* What trust, what relief and what optimism it will give you, in the midst of difficulties, to feel that you are the children of a Father, who knows everything and can do everything.

My children, I *urge you, brothers, to do this more and more, and to aspire to live quietly, and to mind your own affairs, and to work with your hands, as we instructed you, so that you may walk properly before outsiders and be dependent on no one. And let the peace of Christ rule in your hearts.*[99]

Your Father blesses you with all his heart.

---

[99] *Etenim illud facitis in omnes fratres in universa Macedonia. Rogamus autem vos, fratres, ut abundetis magis, et operam detis ut quieti sitis, et ut vestrum negotium agatis, et operemini manibus vestris, sicut praecepimus vobis: et ut honeste ambuletis ad eos, qui foris sunt: et nullius aliquid desideretis* (1 Thess 4:10-12): "For that indeed is what you are doing to all the brothers throughout Macedonia. But we urge you, brothers, to do this more and more, and to aspire to live quietly, and to mind your own affairs, and to work with your hands, as we instructed you, so that you may walk properly before outsiders and be dependent on no one" *Et pax Christi exsultet in cordibus vestris, in qua et vocati estis in uno corpore: et grati estote* (Col 3:15): "And let the peace of Christ rule in your hearts, to which indeed you were called in the one body. And be thankful."

APPENDIX
A CATALOGUE OF THE "COLLECTED LETTERS"

A catalogue is presented below of the 38 *Letters* which St Josemaría had in mind to be printed in 13 volumes. They are numbered using as a reference the date given by the author; the topic covered by each *Letter* is indicated.

The number of pages in each document will offer an idea of the length of each one compared with the others. This figure corresponds to the 1985 edition printed in connection with the Cause of Beatification and Canonisation of the founder.

A detailed Introduction is available in Volume One of this "Collection".

- *Letter* 1: on the call to holiness and apostolate in ordinary life: designated by the opening words *Singuli dies* and is dated 24 March 1930; 23 pages.
- *Letter* 2: on the importance of humility in one's spiritual life: designated by the opening words *Videns eos* and is dated 24 March 1931; 58 pages.
- *Letter* 3: on the supernatural and apostolic mission of the members of Opus Dei in the middle of the world: designated by the opening words *Res omnes* and is dated 9 January 1932; 83 pages.
- *Letter* 4: on the way of proclaiming Christian doctrine through personal apostolate: designated by the opening words *Vos autem* and is dated 16 July 1933; 32 pages.

- *Letter* 5: deals with mission of Opus Dei and of lay Christians in the field of education and teaching: designated by the opening words *Euntes ergo* and is dated 2 October 1939; 31 pages.
- *Letter* 6: is about the characteristic traits of the calling to Opus Dei and its evangelising mission, in the service of the Church: designated by the opening words *Sincerus est* and is dated 11 March 1940; 61 pages.
- *Letter* 7: on the work of St Raphael, for the Christian formation of young people: designated by the opening words *Quem per annos* and is dated 24 October 1942; 54 pages.
- *Letter* 8: deals with the theme of freedom in temporal matters and the spirit of service which characterises the life of members of Opus Dei: designated by the opening words *Legitima hominum* and is dated 31 May 1943; 41 pages.
- *Letter* 9: deals with the juridical solution which allowed priests to be in Opus Dei, coming from the ranks of the lay members: designated by the opening words *Opus nostrum* and is dated 14 February 1944; 19 pages.
- *Letter* 10: on the particular mission of priests in Opus Dei: designated by the opening words *Sacerdotes iam* and is dated 2 February 1945; 34 pages.
- *Letter* 11: deals with spiritual, professional, human and doctrinal formation in Opus Dei: designated by the opening words *Divinus magister* and is dated 6 May 1945; 43 pages.
- *Letter* 12: on the apostolate of public opinion, as a service to God and to men and women, through working in the world of communications: designated by the opening words *Numquam antehac* and is dated 30 April 1946; 67 pages.
- *Letter* 13: explains the misunderstandings and calumnies

with which some people tried to make the pathway of the Work difficult, more specifically throughout its juridical itinerary: designated by the opening words *Ascendente eo,* and it is the only one which carries two dates: 29 December 1947 and 14 February 1966; 209 pages.

- *Letter* 14: deals with professional work, as a specific means of attaining sanctity: designated by the opening words *Meum gaudium* and is dated 15 October 1948; 33 pages.
- *Letter* 15: on the occasion of the definitive pontifical approval of the Work, within the framework of the legislation on Secular Institutes, it explains that being in Opus Dei requires virtues, above all; specifically, dwelling on the consideration of the theological virtues and highlighting their importance in the spirit of the Work: designated by the opening words *Perfice gressus* and is dated 8 December 1949; 242 pages.
- *Letter* 16: on the professional vocation of the members of Opus Dei and support for the apostolic works: designated by the opening words *Bene nostis* and is dated 14 February 1950; 13 pages.
- *Letter* 17: reflecting on the ambiguity of legislation on the figure of Secular Institutes and their evolution, exhorts proceeding with fidelity to the spirit of the Work: designated by the opening words *Via deflectit* and is dated 7 October 1950; 55 pages.
- *Letter* 18: on the theological formation of the faithful of Opus Dei: designated by the opening words *Hac nostra aetate* and is dated 9 January 1951; 18 pages.
- *Letter* 19: refers to the criticisms and calumnies suffered by Opus Dei throughout its history, exhorting understanding and forgiving those who have spread them, but without

failing to make the truth known: designated by the opening words *Hoc tempore* and is dated 14 September 1951; 53 pages.

- *Letter* 20: extended development of the topic of the cardinal virtues, and their importance in the spirit of Opus Dei, as a continuation of *Letter* 15; it contains explanations of the difficulties suffered throughout the history of the Work: designated by the opening words *In patientia* and is dated 24 December 1951; it was thoroughly revised and completed in 1975; 383 pages.
- *Letter* 21: on the evolution which the figure of Secular Institutes was undergoing and the differences from Opus Dei, it deals with secularity, the sanctification of professional work, the freedom and responsibility of the members of the Work regarding temporal matters: designated by the opening words *Multa scripta* and is dated 12 December 1952; 51 pages.
- *Letter* 22: deals with the specific aim of Opus Dei in the context of the mission of the Church; unity and diversity in the way of taking part in this mission: designated by the opening words *Mirabilis omnino* and is dated 15 August 1953; 23 pages.
- *Letter* 23: the theme is the need to preserve and express clearly the complete secularity of the calling of members of the Work: designated by the opening words *Vocationis vestrae* and is dated 19 March 1954; 32 pages.
- *Letter* 24: deals with the differences between the religious state and the spirit of Opus Dei, whose essential traits it describes: designated by the opening words *Sicut antea* and is dated 31 May 1954; 38 pages.
- *Letter* 25: on the characteristics of the work of priests in Opus Dei: designated by the opening words *Divinus*

seminator and is dated 28 March 1955; 27 pages.

- *Letter* 26: deals with the way of carrying out the priestly ministry in Opus Dei: designated by the opening words *Ad serviendum* and is dated 8 August 1956; 50 pages.
- *Letter* 27: on the work of St Michael: the formation of the numeraries and associates and their cooperation in the tasks of formation and governance of Opus Dei: designated by the opening words *Multum usum* and is dated 29 September 1957; 68 pages.
- *Letter* 28: on the juridical situation of Opus Dei, which *de facto* is not a secular institute, although it is so in law: designated by the opening words *Non ignoratis* and is dated 2 October 1958; 7 pages.
- *Letter* 29: on the work of St Gabriel: the vocation of supernumeraries and their mission in the sanctification of the world and of their matrimonial and family life: designated by the opening words *Dei amore* and is dated 9 January 1959; 59 pages.
- *Letter* 30: deals with the dispositions which someone should have, who is going to change country so as to expand the work of Opus Dei: designated by the opening words *Dei voluntas* and is dated 16 June 1960; 30 pages.
- *Letter* 31: explains particular aspects of the secular vocation in Opus Dei, within the framework of the juridical history of the Work: designated by the opening words *Gratias Deo* and is dated 25 January 1961; 73 pages.
- *Letter* 32: explains the need for a change in the juridical configuration of Opus Dei, one that respects the reality of its spirit and of its life; it offers considerations on some of the difficulties and misunderstandings in the history of its juridical itinerary: designated by the opening words *Ne proiicias* and is dated 25 May 1962; 90 pages.

- *Letter* 33: is an exhortation to faithfulness to the Magisterium of the Church: designated by the opening words *Optime nostis* and is dated 2 October 1963; 11 pages.
- *Letter* 34: gives impetus to safeguarding unity with the Magisterium in theological and philosophical research: designated by the opening words *In Opere Dei* and is dated 14 February 1964; 10 pages.
- *Letter* 35: deals with true renewal of Christian life and of the Church, in faithfulness to the Magisterium, in the light of some doctrinal and practical deviations: designated by the opening words *Veritatem facientes* and is dated 15 August 1964; 93 pages.
- *Letter* 36: on the sanctification of the work of the women of Opus Dei, in particular referring to domestic work and the care of the Centres of the Work: designated by the opening words *Verba Domini* and is dated 29 July 1965; 59 pages.
- *Letter* 37: on dialogue: designated by the opening words *Argentum electum* and is dated 24 October 1965; 77 pages.
- *Letter* 38: on the central points of Christian dogma and morals, which St Josemaría wished to remind the members of Opus Dei clearly: designated by the opening words *Fortes in fide* and is dated 19 March 1967; 191 pages.

INDEX TO SACRED SCRIPTURE TEXTS

Note: References are to Paragraph Number

Old Testament

New Testament

SUBJECT INDEX